COMBAT IN THE EROGENOUS ZONE

COMBAT IN THE EROGENOUS ZONE

Ingrid Bengis

With a new Foreword by
Martin Duberman

HarperPerennial
A Division of HarperCollins*Publishers*

This book was originally published in 1972 by Alfred A. Knopf, Inc. It is here reprinted by arrangement with Alfred A. Knopf, Inc.

First HarperPerennial edition published 1991.

LIBRARY OF CONGRESS CATALOGING-IN-PUBLICATION DATA

Bengis, Ingrid.
Combat in the erogenous zone / Ingrid Bengis : with a new foreword by Martin Duberman.
p. cm.
Reprint. Originally published: New York : Knopf, 1972.
ISBN 0-06-097422-2 (pbk.)
1. Lesbianism—United States. 2. Sex (Psychology). 3. Sex differences (Psychology). 4. Bengis, Ingrid. I. Title.
HQ75.6.U5B46 1991
155.3—dc20 91-55112

---

91 92 93 94 95 RRD 10 9 8 7 6 5 4 3 2 1

To Rubin, for helping to create the woman
capable of writing this book.
To Steve, for being himself and believing in me.
To both of them, for showing me that all men
are not necessarily created equal . . .

"... that is what learning is. You suddenly understand something you've understood all your life, but in a new way. There's a pressure on us all the time to go on to something that seems new because there are new words attached to it. But I want to take words as ordinary as bread. Or life. Or death. Cliches. I want to have my nose rubbed in cliches."

DORIS LESSING,
The Four-Gated City

Contents

Foreword xi

Introduction to the HarperPerennial Edition xvii

Introduction 1

Man-Hating 9

Lesbianism 121

Love 201

Foreword

by Martin Duberman*

Ingrid Bengis was only twenty-eight when *Combat in the Erogenous Zone* was originally published in 1972, but she had lived so intensely and could describe her experience so freshly (so free of the "theories and philosophies" she scorned as "much easier to wear than a life") that her ruminations about love, hate, and sex struck many of us who were older than she as astonishingly vivid and wise. Twenty years later, they still do.

Combat is a book that emerged from the ethos of the sixties yet—like anything good of its kind—transcends it. Bengis's emphases and assumptions were those widely shared by the radical young. She regarded her life as an experiment and especially her affective life. Following the mandate of the day, she devoted herself to the search for "authenticity"—of self and of self in relation to others.

*Martin Duberman is Distinguished Professor of History at The Graduate Center/Lehman College, CUNY. His many books include *Black Mountain: An Experiment in Community, Paul Robeson, About Time: Exploring the Gay Past,* and his recent memoir, *CURES.*

She believed that the "truth" of the inner life existed and that it could be uncovered if one were clear-eyed enough to reject the cultural categories that inhibit, homogenize, and violate experience, brave enough to remain rigorously honest with oneself, and open enough to act on the possibilities for self-creation. Again like a good child of the sixties, Bengis had faith in the power, importance, and possibility of communication. And she took as axiomatic the obligation to send back messages from the front, to employ the knowledge gained from her interior skirmishes for broader social purposes.

Experience tempered those beliefs. Her inability to get most men, even those who claimed to love her, to acknowledge her full humanity, to understand her basic needs, to respond other than superficially to her patient attempts at intimate communication, produced in her a bitterness and confusion that in some moods led her to label herself a man-hater. Some of the most eloquent pages in *Combat* recount her experiences with genuinely nice men who abused her emotionally, and with a noncomprehending casualness that made her fiercely resentful.

The dynamics of male/female interaction that Bengis described some twenty years ago remain powerfully intact. Indeed, today the dynamics may be more pronounced than ever, now that so many men have grown indifferent to feminist analysis, and so many others have settled for dutifully mouthing the rhetoric of feminism without making any sustained effort to apply it to their own lives. There is nothing dated, alas, in Bengis's description of the "liberated" male's "self-righteous generosity" toward the women of his acquaintance, and his expectation that they will be grateful for his sympathy. Bengis calls the liberated male's attitude "packaged comprehension"—the assumption that someone with a different life experience can be easily and quickly understood, without any real willingness to open and change oneself.

Her analysis, of course, applies to differentness of all kinds. And she herself explicitly—and for 1972 daringly—applies it to the reaction of "progressive" straight people (herself included, sometimes) to gays and lesbians: they learn a few words that suggest understanding, apply a little patronizing sympathy that safely keeps the Other at a distance. Herself passionately involved with her own gender, Bengis nonetheless is frightened when she sometimes finds herself drawn more irresistibly than usual to a particular woman. Able to acknowledge that she is terrified at the intensity of her feelings for "Dee," the woman she shares an apartment with, Bengis becomes fearful that she might herself be that despised thing, a lesbian. Her honest anguish as she wrestles with her own ambivalent attractions is deeply moving.

Though she keeps herself open to new experience, Bengis does not close herself off to some old emotional truths. *Un*fashionably (for the sixties), she rejects the "ersatz progressivism" that pretends erotic adventuring is a more insistent concern, finally, than ordinary love. She is a passionate defender of the centrality of our need for comfort, and brilliantly argues for the view that monogamy, not multiplicity, provides it—indeed even argues that having continuity in a relationship may be precisely what makes spontaneity possible in the rest of our lives.

Combat has its problems. Bengis waffles uncertainly on the issue of whether male/female differences are biological in origin. We all do this, of course, but some of us don't come down, as Bengis seems to, on the side of men being *innately* inclined to multiple relationships and women (following Erik Erikson's notion, popular in the sixties) being *inherently* driven, as a result of their relationship to gestation, to fill a "complex inner space" with an emotional connection. Given her love for women and her distrust of men, moreover, Bengis is, predictably, more sympathetic to lesbians than to gay men, and is especially repelled by swishy gay men, who she seems to feel are parodying women rather than (a more common view today) simply being themselves.

Occasionally, too, Bengis's portrayed emotions border on the merely theatrical. She sometimes thrashes around with such prideful intensity—she breaks out in cold sweats, she vomits, she trembles, she faints—that she seems to be melodramatically heightening her own experience. But that may simply be because she is more finely tuned than most of us. In any case, her nerve endings seem so raw that for some readers the book's tumultuous pitch will at times produce distrust and exhaustion.

Far more frequently, Bengis rings emotionally true—and appealing: brave and vulnerable, subtle, generous, and smart. And her prose achieves an Isherwood-like transparency (without his guarded need for distance), a lucidness and clarity, that powerfully conveys the possibilities and difficulties of human contact, which is her central, enduring theme.

Introduction to the HarperPerennial Edition

I was twenty-six years old when I wrote *Combat in the Erogenous Zone,* and I remember very clearly the period shortly after it was published, now twenty years ago, when I was often asked to speak to students at universities around the country. The theme from the book which both disturbed and attracted them the most was "Man-Hating," and it was obvious that they had come to these gatherings expecting the author to resemble the theme. Their astonishment when I walked into the room, looking and sounding considerably softer than they expected, was almost palpable. They waited for me to snarl, to speak caustically to the men and solicitously to the women, or not to speak to the men at all, but in this as in many other things, I failed to live up (or down) to their expectations, though in truth I was as often surprised by them as they were by me. In particular I was surprised by the men, since the ones who came to listen and participate were often so gentle, introspective, and even contrite without having anything noticeable to be contrite about, that I was at times more afraid for their futures than for my own, and more than once a vast maternal tenderness entangled my speech in response to their anguish. I wanted to say to them, don't worry, it's OK, you're not the ones I had in mind at all, you never could be, but the words dissolved in my mouth, and I was left with the image of their nervousness over the prospect of unintentionally harming women of whom they were fond, their fear of their own desires and their sensitivity which sometimes bordered on paralysis. What I saw in them was a danger quite different from the danger which I confronted in the book, a danger of suppressing themselves to the point of obliteration, of losing themselves entirely. Although they were in a state of acute apprehension when they first entered the room, often by the time the gatherings were over, they had revealed their vulnerabilities in a way which elicited my own as well, so that I found myself having the kinds of heartfelt dialogues with them which in the past had seemed virtually impossible. It occurred to me then that I was witnessing the ripening of a new generation of young men with distinctly altered sensibilities who were obliging me to revise my responses to them, as well as to revise the views which I had expressed in the book. What did I think of these young men? I wasn't sure. The question was perplexing.

About six months earlier, during the interregnum between the time when I finished writing *Combat* and the time when it was published, I was living on the Lower East Side of New York and working at a variety of odd jobs which included posing as an artist's model in exchange for free art classes. In retrospect I suspect that my decision to model had something to do with an attempt to neutralize my own sexuality, and I did, in fact, feel so safe doing it that during the sustained periods of silence when I was posing I often drifted off into a reverie, mentally disappearing from the room altogether to concentrate on conjuring up entire paragraphs of prose in my mind. My ability to sustain a pose for long periods of time without becoming restless or uncomfortable was largely due to my mental absence from the scene, but it made me a good model, frequently in demand.

At that time no one among my acquaintances, or even among my friends, knew very much about the book which I had just finished writing, and from the outside at least, my life appeared to be freewheeling, brave, and experimental. Since I had always been an intensely private person, more inclined to intellectual philosophizing than personal self-revelation, the people with whom I surrounded myself also often didn't know what I felt, and when an agitated young man came over to speak to me at the end of one class, it was obvious that he didn't either. He was a university senior and quite painfully shy, though his drawings of me, oddly enough, were concentrated almost exclusively, sometimes even comically, on the erogenous zones. In a halting voice he confessed with considerable embarrassment that over the past year he had become obsessed with women's bodies. He was a virgin, he said, and terrified of spoiling his friendships with women by trying to sleep with any of them. On the other hand, this fear seemed to be making him a virtual slave to his sexual drive, and the crisis had reached the point where he could think of nothing else. For weeks, he said, he had been watching me with intense interest and had concluded from his observations that I was both experienced and kind. Would I be willing to sleep with him so that he could become a normal man? He was so distressed that it was impossible to laugh or to tell him that things like this only happened in books like the one I happened to have just finished writing. But of course he didn't know that I was a writer, nor did I have any desire to tell him. Let me emphasize at this point that I did not feel in the least offended by his request, perhaps because I recognized something of him in myself, perhaps because he was so obviously terrified, and perhaps also because he was unaware that I might detect in the possibility of this encounter something potentially healing, not only for him but also for myself. I said nothing about any of this though. I just said yes, wondering if I would know what to do, since I myself was a good deal less experienced than I appeared to be and certainly less experienced than many former readers of this book seemed to believe. Looking back on that time, I still feel that I was right to accept his proposal, and I have never regretted doing so, for the experience did in fact teach me something about mutual fragility, taught me that it was possible to heal each other through a sort of willed self-exposure, to make of our fear and desperation an asset rather than a liability, to grow. I never did tell him my full name, and he wasn't aware until much later than I had written this book. When he found out, he was overcome with remorse, but it was a remorse which I didn't share and I told him so. Ultimately, we became friends, though we never slept with each other again, and he never did know that it would be almost ten years before I slept with anyone else either. For that, at least, I am grateful.

During a substantial portion of the twenty years since I finished writing this book, I have been unable to look at it, let alone read it. When I finally did force myself to reread it in anticipation of its being reissued, I was actually surprised to discover that it was much better than I had expected. In those days, of course, I had a fairly large number of opinions about life and my own experiences, some of which I agree with today, and others which I consider excessive, but I suspect that if you don't have a lot of opinions when you are twenty-six there is something wrong with you. I have fewer opinions today at the age of forty-six, but they seem to be just as strongly held as my earlier ones, and this too is probably typical for my age. Fortunately for me though, this is a book which is filled with contradictions, contradictions of which I think I can be justifiably proud, for they, rather than the opinions, are the book's backbone and the primary source of my not unpleasant sense of surprise when I first began to examine the former self who still lives in these pages.

This said, I nonetheless have to confess that the moment I stepped back from this book for more than a few minutes, I once again felt as ill at ease and at times even as shocked by it as I have been ever since the moment when

I first sat down at the typewriter to write it. Or rather, ever since the moment when I found myself putting into words thoughts and feelings which were almost impossible to associate with the self whom I had more or less come to know and like during the first twenty-five years of my life. For the truth is that for me at least, this book has always been an albatross, and it still is.

Of course it is common enough for writers to look back on their early work with a certain sense of embarrassment and dismay, perhaps tempered by indulgence, and if they don't, chances are that they either didn't grow, or never developed a capacity for critical self-examination. *Combat* is something of a special case though, because it is so intensely personal and so clearly locked into states of mind associated with a particular period in my life, which once it was over, I much preferred to consider "part of my past" rather than "part of my present." The primary function of nostalgia is to enable us to gloss over our own personal history, and one of the problems with this book for me is that it makes nostalgia and its corresponding revisions virtually impossible.

Perhaps as a way of dealing with this dilemma, I developed the habit, soon after the book was published, of thinking of the person who appears in it and who had all those awful feelings as a "she," a persona, rather than a "me," my real self. This attitude was to some extent made possible by the fact that I had clearly emphasized the problematic sides of my life, its dark and uncomfortable underbelly, at the expense of those sides with which it was easier to live. The result as I saw it, was a sort of quasi-fictional character, a distortion of myself in the service of truth.

Of course the book was never intended to present a pretty portrait of myself. Its purpose was rather to purge myself of thoughts, feelings, and experiences, many of which I found personally distasteful, and if the success of a book like this can be measured (for the author of it, at least) in terms of the extent to which, by the act of its completion, it ceases to be true for the person who wrote it, then *Combat* was a rousing success for me, clearing the decks, freeing me from parts of myself which I found both frightening and unacceptable. Judging from the number of letters I received in response to it (and to my permanent regret, felt incapable of answering), it had a similar cathartic effect on its readers.

Yet, if as I have just said, the writing of this book succeeded in freeing me from it, why am I still uncomfortable with it, why does it still seem to demand an ongoing confrontation with myself, why have I so frequently over the years taken refuge in dismissing it . . . my own, my first child . . . as "a product of its time" and dated? Why do I, when asked about what I have written, try to avoid "confessing" that yes, indeed, I am the woman who wrote that book way back then, the one whose title might ring a bell in your mind . . . the one (and at this point my voice usually diminishes to a near whisper) called *Combat in the Erogenous Zone?*

Frequently the jaw drops just a little. *You wrote that?* they say. Why, I remember that book. Umm . . . well, yes I did write it, I say. *But it was a long time ago.* And I would much prefer to have written *War and Peace* or even *Notes from Underground* or the poems of Akhmatova.

But I loved that book, they say. I kept it next to the bed when my husband and I were going through a difficult period in our marriage. We read it out loud to each other. I underlined a lot of passages. It was great. It really helped me.

Yes, I say again in a whisper, with an air of dejection. I'm glad.

What's the matter? they say with profound astonishment. Aren't you proud of it?

It's dated, I say, taking a certain comfort in being able to put a neat parenthesis around my own feelings and thoughts, as if by capturing them on the run I could thereby pacify them into submission for eternity.

Well, that's true in some ways but . . .

No buts, I say firmly, closing the subject and thinking, thank god I don't have to talk about *that* again.

But whether or not I have to talk about it, the book is still there, and when I begin to consider the possibility of its being brought back to life again, hauled out of mothballs by someone who seems to believe that it *isn't* dated, I am forced to examine it all over again, to say to myself, hey, wake up, you wrote this thing, so look at it. Maybe it's not your favorite child, maybe you had it out of wedlock, maybe it has a cleft palate, but it's *yours.* Besides, ideas can be dated, but not feelings, and the kinds of feelings which do become dated are not really feelings at all, but ideas about feelings, a very different kettle of fish.

It is easy enough after all, to recant or to alter ideas. A

life, on the other hand, is not quite so malleable. What it was, it was, and its vitality and tragedy cannot be revised even by a mind which may, in fact, long to do so. Such, I must confess, was and is my mind. So that when I admit that in some way I wish I had never written this book, I have to acknowledge as well that what I am really saying is: I wish a lot of these things had never happened to me, I wish I could forget about them, I wish I had never felt what I did, I wish I could say it wasn't true. Fortunately or unfortunately, however, this book is or was true . . . with or without its persona, with or without its datedness . . . but deep down, somewhere inside of myself, I continue to wish that it wasn't, wish furthermore that instead of writing this new introduction, I could simply revise the book altogether, and thereby revise my life to make it conform more precisely to my tastes as they exist today and to some extent, as they existed even then. I wish I could believe that it really is dated. I wish it would disappear.

The present reader should therefore be warned not to count me as one of this book's ardent admirers. Count me rather as a wary skeptic, as one of those ambivalent people who has spent twenty years resisting this book, one of those people who read it and said, "Oh come on Ingrid, did you really think that? Did you really feel that? Weren't you exaggerating ever so slightly? And why did you set yourself up for that situation in the first place? Didn't you know that you were asking for trouble? Didn't you realize?"

At the heart of such speculation, such skepticism, is a much deeper question that arises as a result of having lived the life which I attempted to describe in these pages, a question which nagged at me during the writing of this book and nags at me still. That question is "Could I or should I have lived my life differently, so that these things which 'happened' to me during the first twenty-five years of my life could have been avoided, so that I would not have had to pay the price I ultimately did pay for exposing myself so readily to life's hazards, even seeming at times to court them?" For of course I did pay for that exposure, not only during the period described in *Combat* but also for years after, paid with at least ten years of a life lived under conditions of the most extremely chaste asceticism, counter-balancing my earlier excessiveness with a corresponding restraint which was at times almost monastic. So while it is true that writing *Combat* was cathartic in the most immediate sense, it is also true that the cumulative emotional effects of my experiences went much deeper than I could have imagined at the time of the book's writing. The pure excess was vented, never to return, but the rest was not, though the book, by making me more outwardly vulnerable than I ever had been before, also made me more self-protective in the future. All this should not really be surprising though. The critical scarring events of a life, any life, are like internal nuclear accidents, Three Mile Islands, Chernobyls of the spirit, in which the immediate fallout, while it can be startling and dramatic, hardly ever matches the long term damage whose effects are impossible to estimate, calculate, or even fully comprehend.

One of the most pervasive illusions of American life is

that it is possible to live a life without consequences. Even if our families raise us to believe otherwise, struggling to sustain through us the values which they have carried with them through life, still the seduction of a seemingly celestial and limitless freedom is omnipresent, luring us into the optimistic belief that we can afford collective historical amnesia and dilettantism and the squandering of inner resources. We can change our lives the way we change our clothes. We can have it all. But the effect of this on an individual psyche (not even considering its effects on the national psyche) is corrosive, making it extremely difficult for any of us to stop long enough to ask ourselves critical long-range questions about responsibility, meaning, and purpose, questions which every society must ask itself if it intends to survive spiritually. For there is no such thing as not paying a price. The only question is, How much, when, for how long, and is it worth it?

Buried somewhere inside this book is precisely that question: How much, when, for how long? And it is only now, looking back on the period which this book describes as well as on the one which followed it that I can begin to ask myself: my god, was all this necessary? My god, was it worth it?

Obviously this is not an idle question, either for me or for anyone who undertakes to read this book for the first time. If none of it was necessary and none of it was worth it, then why read the book in the first place, except as an atlas of disaster, a roadmap indicating the routes to avoid, a cautionary tale of the sort mothers traditionally tell their young daughters in order to prepare them for the pitfalls which lie ahead, with examples and illustrations of what can befall them if they don't choose the path of righteous caution? Is this a morality tale, a piece of social history or a confessional monologue? Is it, as many people in the small town where I spent my teenage years believed, a "dirty book?" Is it the memoir of a man-hater or a romantic, a feminist or a traditionalist, a conservative or a radical? Is it personal or political or both? Is it a bildungsroman or a picaresque tale or just the story of a woman's life gone slightly haywire? Is it all of the above? Does it have a point, and if so, what is it? Are there any lessons at all to be learned from it? Was I a casualty, along with so many women of my generation, of my conditioning or a casualty of my character? Was I (were we) casualties at all?

Let me say at this point that although *Combat* was warmly embraced by feminists, I did not, at the time I wrote it, think of myself as a feminist. I had never been part of a consciousness raising group, nor had I read any feminist literature, and when I try to recollect whether or not I knew anyone who considered themselves a feminist, no one at all comes to mind. Given my lifelong penchant for softness and femininity, my love of it, many feminists would probably have seemed frightening to me. Furthermore, being a feminist would have required me to have some collective sense of my own condition, and that in itself might have eased the sense of direct confrontation with myself which the writing of this book provoked. I didn't feel that I was carrying a banner in the name of freedom; I felt that I was a weirdo, with my anger, my sentimentality and Victorian morality, my personal eccentricity, flamboyance and hypersensitive pride.

The fact is that I have always been incapable of long remaining a participant in any movement, even one launched on my own behalf, even one which would grant me that elusive sense of belonging which I always thought I craved. The renegade in me was too strong, the devil's advocate too ingenious, and even though I agreed, and still agree, with a substantial number of feminist perceptions, I nonetheless inwardly rebel against considering myself a feminist, if only out of a perverse sort of contrariness, an inability to believe that any world view can completely define an individual's existence, an unwillingness to expunge the telling detail which invariably upsets the most compelling of theories. Ultimately, I am not a theoretician, and I have consistently been more attracted to the ragtag piece of information which throws a theory awry than I am to the predictable one which confirms it, regardless of what the theory may be. That is why I usually prefer fiction to nonfiction, contradiction to consistency, and it is probably why I felt such a profound sense of relief when one day recently, while reading Nikolai Berdaev's *Slavery and Freedom,* I came across the following:

> Change destroys personality when it is transformed into treason . . . One can change one's view about where and how freedom of the spirit is realized. But if love of freedom is replaced by love of servitude and violence, then treason is the result . . . I think that man is after all, an inconsistent and polarized being . . . The

end of this dynamic of the spirit and its ever newly arising contradictions can only be the end of the world. Until the world ends, contradictions cannot be abolished . . .

That does not, of course, mean that it is impossible to have beliefs, or to engage in social action, but only that the validity of that action is not based on fixed realities but rather on something fluid and unpredictable and often ambiguous . . . on life.

Further on in the same book, Berdaev elaborates on the particular contradictions in his own nature, contradictions which are so closely related to the conflicts in *Combat,* which is also to say, the conflicts in me, that I think they are worth quoting again:

The fundamental contradiction in my thinking about social life is bound up with the juxtaposition in me of two elements—an artistocratic interpretation of personality, freedom and creativeness, and a socialistic demand for the assertion of the dignity of every man, of even the most insignificant of men, and for a guarantee of his rights in life. This is the clash of a passionate love of the world above, of a love of the highest, with pity for this lower world, the world of suffering. This contradiction is age-long . . .

When a levelling tyranny offends against my understanding of the dignity of personality, my love of freedom and creativeness, I rebel against it and I am ready to express my revolt in the extremest form. But when the defenders of social inequality shamelessly defend their own privileges and turn a man into a thing, then also I rebel. In both cases, I reject the foundations of the contemporary world.*

I suspect that this conflict has meaning for virtually every intelligent human being of conscience, but it may be particularly meaningful for women, because the expression of personality, freedom, and creativeness is, in most societies, granted to men more easily than to women, and women who assume that right for themselves generally find themselves paying not only the price which is exacted from every human being who strikes out into the world as an individual with a certain number of heroic fantasies but also the additional price associated with a woman's particular sexual vulnerability.

At the age of twenty-six, however, this was something which I had clearly failed to understand. I identified so strongly with Berdaev's point of view, and was so much of a nineteenth-century romantic, that it never occurred to me that I was doing anything other than living the life of a creative person who believed passionately in social equality, but also perceived myself as being outside of or in some way above the question of social equality in the living out of my own personal destiny. Maybe other people needed social equality, but surely not me. The role of victim, a role which I found repugnant, would never be mine. Given these feelings, I was thus somewhat shocked

*Although Berdaev uses the word "man" throughout this quote, he wrote in Russian and Russian does not have this problem of gender to indicate "humanity" as male.

and bewildered to discover the consequences of my own vulnerability and equally astonished that my enthusiasm for life had led me into a cul de sac from which no forward progress seemed possible, though I was nonetheless convinced that this was merely a stage which I would pass through on my way to the "future." As an adventurer, enthusiast, and idealist, I couldn't grasp the fact that my wings had somehow been broken by the mere fact of spontaneously exposing myself to life in ways which seemed to me exhilarating, even when they were painful. Was this because I was a woman? Because of social inequality? It seemed absolutely inconceivable to me. I had done everything I wanted to do after all. No one had been able to stop me, not even society with its well-intentioned warnings. Anyone who wanted to live freely could, and if they didn't it was their own fault, it was because they didn't have the grit and stamina and determination and energy. I, on the other hand . . .

Thinking back on it, I see all too clearly that I hadn't really come to terms yet with the idea of consequences, perhaps because I was so much in the thick of living them out that I was unable to recognize them for what they were. I just thought that I was living through one phase and would then proceed to the next, like going from one chapter of a book to another in which the point of view shifts, and the story takes on a whole other hue. So that although my emotional life had come to a grinding halt, my ideas about my own future, what it should and would become, still revolved around certain fixed poles, and it didn't actually occur to me that the consequences of the present would carry forward into the future. I thought that my future was something I would find, and that would be the end of it. I didn't perceive it as being something which was continuous with the present. In fact, until I was almost forty, I believed despite the fact that all the evidence of my life seemed to mitigate against it, that any day now I would find myself in a house with a wonderful husband and five children and we would all sit around the dining room eating the bountiful meals which I had just prepared from scratch for an extended family consisting of aunts, uncles, parents, and assorted friends who congregated to talk about life in the manner of characters in a Chekhov play. Like those characters, I refused to surrender my illusions. I preferred to believe in an idyllic future which never had and never would exist but which, in my mind's eye, was the only ideal worth pursuing; I believed that one fine morning I would wake up knowing where home was, wake up on the right road, the road which all too clearly was the road not taken, wake up with a life neatly divided into two parts with the first part a shining example of adventure and glory and the second, well . . . normal.

Even when I found myself in the midst of a third part—what I might call the stage of consequences—I didn't recognize that it had any bearing at all on my design for the future. Maybe I was just putting it off a little, that was all. A little . . . a little more . . . a little.

Obviously it took me an exceptionally long time to understand that the parts had something to do with the whole, that while I was waiting for my future to happen, it had already happened, that the whole thing was continuous, and if not consecutive then at least derived from the consequences of what had preceded it, and that the life which I have "ended up with" (but the future is always ahead of us, even now), was not an accident at all, and that if I am a casualty of anything, it is of a not uncommon tendency to prefer fantasy to fact. Ultimately then, I have to admit that one of the reasons why I am and always have been so uncomfortable with this book is not because it is dishonest but rather because it is too honest, because it has succeeded in pinning me like a butterfly to truths which, on my own, without the benefit of this book, I would probably have faced only intermittently, and even then with the utmost reluctance. I am uncomfortable because it spotlights for me that I am who I am today at least in part because of who I was then, and it is impossible for me to pretend that away. The book itself is the evidence, the proof, and ultimately perhaps the only weapon against my own nostalgia for a way of life and an experience which I had always imagined for myself, in contrast to the life which I actually ended up having.

Is this a good thing or a bad thing? For if the book forces me to look at uncomfortable truths, then it should also enable me to assess those truths, and to ask with greater clarity those questions with which I began this introduction. If I don't have the luxury of blurring the past, then clearly I must come to terms with the present, acknowledging to myself that the strengths which are contained in this book, a certain merciless drive to self-exposure, a seemingly relentless capacity for self-questioning, and the vulnerability of a survivor are strengths which are still with me and still of use to me. They are strengths which were developed, at least in part, as a result of the struggle to master those experiences which I could not control as well as those which I could have controlled but didn't. Maybe they are not strengths which can be worn easily. Maybe they will itch and rub into eternity. But they are mine. They belong to me. And while many things may have been lost along the way, they have not. That at least, has not been one of the consequences.

Am I then, or am I not, a casualty? The answer, despite everything I have said previously is no, though all of us who have taken risks with our lives have certain scars to show for those risks. The casualty is rather my own hubris, my youthful faith in regard to my capacity to erase from an emerging character the cumulative signs of the past. And yet, knowing all that, when I look at the person I have become, I see that while I did not become the inhabitant of an ivory tower, did not become what I thought I should become and what I once wished to become, I did become something else: a reasonably independent woman without regrets, with a large number of my capacities intact, a woman who has managed to live according to my principles, with few compromises, a woman who has paid the price, survived, and grown up. For there is no such thing as a life without a price, and anyone who has reached the age of forty and believes that there is, is either lying to themselves or has simply refused to live at all. Could it have been lesser or smaller? I doubt it. Different, yes, but if the outcome so far has been better than might have been expected under the circumstances, then why quibble?

So yes I paid the price, and yes it was worth it. The spontaneous joy which sometimes surges up in me at the knowledge that I circumvented the truly tragic outcomes which arise from living someone else's life rather than one's own is in itself liberating. Knowing that makes me feel considerably lighter, though I can still sometimes be saddened when I think of the thwarted potentials in myself as well as in most of the people I know and love. But coming to terms with consequences means taking responsibility for one's own past, claiming it and moving on. Rereading this book and trying to accept the person in it has made me see that this is a task which, to some extent, still lies ahead of me.

INGRID BENGIS
February 26, 1991
The Writers Room

Introduction

When I first started writing this book, I thought I had a great many ideas about women, other women as well as myself. There were, I believed, general principles of experience that could be applied to women, general attitudes that characterized men. It was the general principles that defined the meaning of our collective existences. Except each time I set out to record these general principles, to part the waters dividing men and women, faces would bob to the surface of my imagination, the faces of women I knew well or had merely glimpsed in passing, women I had loved and hated and competed with, faces of men I had been friends with or enemies of. Sometimes, like characters come to life in my mind, their faces grew sad, or accusing, or disbelieving, or sometimes merely questioning.

"Excuse me," I would hear them saying. "Are you sure you're speaking about me? I've heard that a thousand times before, but what does it really mean?" Then they would stand between me and the page urging me to stop for a minute and listen to this story or that story, listen to what they had to say about the time when . . .

Gradually I became more and more frustrated by these interior conversations. It seemed that if I listened to the recollected voices of everyone I knew, I would have absolutely nothing to say or at least nothing truthful. On the other hand, if I listened to none of them, I would end up repeating those cliches and generalizations which had been reiterated so often that they had long ago made *me* feel that I was being mechanistically interpreted, denied the right to live my own life. It was against those generalizations that I had reacted so strongly, since they always seemed to violate my experience . . . and now I was preparing to articulate a new series of generalizations which would in turn violate someone else's experience. Wasn't it the failure of those generalizations to take into account the intricacies and ambiguities of lives and loves that had provoked me to begin articulating my own thoughts in the first place? But if all I could do was replace someone else's generalities with my own, I would end by defending a turf that I might mark off as mine, but that would never really belong to me, since the only turf I could actually defend was one that had no boundaries, one that provided room for the lives of separate individuals—both male and female—choosing separate ways of living: a turf that only shut out the constricting prejudices of theories constructed in advance and applied with monotonous regularity to lives which were infinitely various.

What I could share with others was the fact of a common humanity, a common uncertainty about the absolute meaning of anything, a common search for a decent way to live. What I could share with them was a series of questions, questions to which I had no answers. But beyond that, we were all on our own, living with or without hopes and expectations.

So I began to write a different book, one in which I would speak for myself, and for no one else, a book with which others might or might not identify, might or might not find idiosyncratic or neurotic.

Once I had abandoned the search for everyone else's truth, I quickly discovered that the job of defining my own truth was far more complex than I had anticipated. Nothing, it seemed, could be a matter of simple affirmations, for now, instead of other people's experience demanding my immediate attention, there was my experience, just as various and just as inconsistent. Each of the faces drawn from the lives of others had a counterpart in my own life. Each had staked a claim to some portion of my own psyche. Each external event had a corresponding internal event. If I had something in common with everyone, I had everything in common with no one.

Not only that, but I soon came to realize that the moment an emotion rose to the surface of my imagination, there to meet with some facet of life, I was able to find a thousand pieces of evidence with which to buttress that emotion, a thousand reasons why I felt the way I did, a thousand means of verifying its authenticity. It didn't matter whether the emotion was anger or love or hatred or affection . . . always there were reasons and justifications. My memory provided me with an inexhaustible reservoir of contradictory information. And each piece of information could be interpreted differently, depending on my current perspective, depending just as often on fluctuations of mood. On those days when someone was unnecessarily cruel to me, images of cruelty dominated my thinking. I would see the world as a cruel place, filled with people bent on shattering me. Then, on some other day, I would speak to someone I cared for, or listen to a story about some moment of deep intimacy in the life of a friend, and a new corner of memory, a new way of seeing that memory, would suddenly open itself up.

How then could I possibly trust any of my own ideas? The fact was that I couldn't. Everything could be scrambled and reordered without notice. Even if I told the truth about whatever "happened" at a particular time, there was always some other truth waiting its turn, insisting on its rights. I would tell the story about the time when . . . and then would find myself thinking about another time when the exact opposite had happened with the exact opposite conclusion.

There was no hope then, for telling the truth. In order to do so, I would have to say everything simultaneously, say a thing and its opposite in a single phrase. Since I was unable to do that, the whole picture would always be beyond my grasp.

A partial picture was the best I could expect, a portrait with selected highlights and shadows. I had on occasion wondered, when looking at a famous painting, about what the back side of the subject looked like, wondered how so-and-so appeared when seen from the rear, or what such-and-such a scene would be like when perceived from across the swamp instead of from in front of the mansion. Perspective, it seemed to me, was everything, and perspective could be endlessly various. The discovery that the world was round shook up millions of people who had held complete faith in its flatness. The discovery that human life is round is still shaking up most of us. Everything can be seen from another angle, and if you keep on walking, keep on assimilating the variations of perspective, sooner or later you come back to the beginning, only to realize that there is no beginning, and no end either.

This then is a portrait from several angles. I have tried to acknowledge the part that imperfections of vision play in my own perspective, although admittedly I am unable to see the back of my own head. I have allowed myself what some might call the "luxury" of inconsistency, although I doubt that the kind of uncertainty which inevitably accompanies inconsistency, can ever be a true luxury.

What I am most concerned with is exploring the possibilities for human contact. But I have discovered that in order to achieve such contact, it is first necessary to deal with all of those things which obstruct contact: with the tendency to hatred and destructiveness as it exists in all of us, the need for love and the fear of it, the social barriers, the personal barriers, the desires and frustrations and expectations and disappointments . . . all of those things that turn relations between men and women into a war zone. For myself, I have to deal with the ways in which I, as one human being, am sometimes driven away from precisely what I most desire.

Combat is divided into three sections, perhaps arbitrarily, for the division might lead you to believe that the ideas and feelings expressed in the separate chapters are linear and sequential. They are not. Love, hate, and sexuality, in relation to my own sex and the opposite sex, coexist simultaneously. They are only separated for the purpose of seeing each one more clearly. If you are hoping for conclusions about the possibilities for love and hate among men and women, you will be disappointed. I have none. I cannot even say at what point I "rest." Do I hate men or love them, hate women or love them? Do I reject sex between men and women, women and women, or celebrate and experience it as being inherently contradictory? The answer of course, is yes—to everything. The conflict between love and lust, need and fear, is a perpetual one, and perhaps the only reality that remains firm is the reality of conflict itself . . . one step forward, one step back.

Since new evidence is always appearing, new shifts in the constellations of feeling taking place, I usually have the sense of verging upon several things at once. The only way I can live is by not defining things too precisely, since I have seen how easily we all get trapped in our own categories, our own tendency to try and fit experience into a mold. Therefore I have left all of the doors open, not for the sake of recklessness, but as a matter of fidelity to the fluctuations and irregularities that real life imposes on us. Anything else, it seems to me, leads to the creation of images—of oneself, the culture, society—that destroy our potential for a self-creation which can proceed only if one refuses to set up formulas in advance.

Fundamentally, I suppose it is a question of being true to whatever is most unique and least standardized in each of us. I am in revolt against the "techniques" of living, whether those techniques express "contemporary attitudes" or not. I am opposed to all rules that drain the juices out of existence. I am in search of authenticity, in search of sex and love which reflect that authenticity, and reflect the kind of purity which is reserved for essentials, even when those essentials prove to be less than pleasant. It is a long haul. And this is only the beginning.

More often than not, though, it seems to me that human existence presents us with an endless gallery of grotesques, in which there is a place for everyone and for all kinds of truths. The farther inward I proceed, the more I realize that the examination of inner life reveals as much truth as we are ever capable of discovering. The truth of obsession is as valid as the truth of objectivity and has as much potential for universality, perhaps even more. Both objectivity and obsession (or distortion) are equally part of life, equally grotesque. We know as little about pure objectivity as we know about pure distortion. Most frequently the two commingle in indefinable doses. All I can say is that if you see something of yourself in me, as I have seen something of myself in you, if my distortions are yours as well, then maybe we can begin to reexamine our ideas about distortion. For the time being, I suppose that will have to do as a substitute for the larger truths.

INGRID BENGIS
January 1972
Stonington, Maine

MAN-HATING

"I will hate if I can; if not, I will unwillingly love."

OVID

1

Man-hating is one of the real questions. The real questions are the ones that obtrude upon your consciousness whether you like it or not, the ones that make your mind start vibrating like a jackhammer, the ones that you "come to terms with" only to discover that they are still there. The real questions refuse to be placated. They barge into your life at the times when it seems most important for them to stay away. They are the questions asked most frequently and answered most inadequately, the ones that reveal their true natures slowly, reluctantly, most often against your will. They lie athwart the spirit like giant-thighed shadows pinning it down until it fights back or surrenders. All too often the real questions don't even seem to have any answers. And they gain their substance out of pain.

Man-hating. Even the word sounds omnivorous. It reminds me of sharks, stingrays, octopi and Venus's-flytraps. It sounds very much like man-eating, and makes me shiver with a fear half composed of acquiescence, half composed of a will to denial. "Go away," I say to the creature. But it rises up as though it had a life of its own and refuses to be quieted by a me more accommodating to the exigencies of survival in a world that exists in extremity and yet cannot seem to tolerate extremity.

I don't think I ever chose man-hating to be part of my life. It seems to have chosen me. And no matter how many times I glare at it and yell, "You're ugly and irrational," it doesn't disappear. "It" takes the offensive. Makes a mockery of intelligence. "It" prevents me from leaping into the breach and announcing that only a "lunatic fringe" indulges in the grotesquerie of man-hating. It forces me to confess that I am not part of any lunatic fringe, but that it has nonetheless established a seemingly permanent home inside of me.

If a free choice were really mine, I would say that I am capable of loving men, or at least loving a few of them and liking a good many others, and that my loves and likes have something to do with whether those men are worth being loved or liked. The truth is that I *do* like many men and have thought I loved two or three. But the other truth is that I hate men, both generally and specifically, and that the hatred sometimes threatens to obliterate even the possibilities for love. It is a hatred that can be of demonic, though often repressed, ferocity. Rap sessions can't break the back of it, nor antimale tirades, nor psychoanalysis (at least not so far), nor demonstrations against the oppression of women, nor, for that matter, writing about it.

My will to fight against it, no matter how strong, is sometimes just not strong enough. For it is will that makes me turn to my dreams and dissect them one by one in the hope of finding some decent *reason* for the hatred; it is will that makes me think there has to be *a* reason, as if by so isolating it I might hope to extract it whole.

Man-hating is a defense, a refusal, and an affirmation. It is a defense against fear, against pain. It is a refusal to suppress the evidence of one's experience. It is an affirmation of the cathartic effects of justifiable anger. What is primary is the possibility for release gained from acknowledging its existence, and the renewal that can sometimes accompany its expression. For if I say today, "I hate you," it is in order that tomorrow it might perhaps be easier to say, "I love you."

To that end, what I can do is try to understand more about what provokes man-hating attacks in me, understand when and why it is justified, understand *something*, in short, of what it's all about.

One day a couple of months ago, I stopped by my old apartment, which I had subleased to a friend. We sat and talked for a while, and eventually I got around to telling him that I intended to write about man-hating.

"So now you're a man-hater," my friend said, as though indulging a temporary whim of mine. "Come on . . ."

When I insisted I was serious, he offered a suggestion. "You ought to mention," he said, "that in the first three hours since you've been home, there have been six phone calls from six different men."

"That doesn't have anything to do with it," I protested,

thinking that none of the men who had phoned would describe me as a man-hater either, thinking that unlike that class of men who consider any woman who believes in female rights a man-hater, most of the men I knew would only call a woman a man-hater if she reacted with constant, overt, and aggressive expressions of venom toward all men. My friend, on the other hand, would be more strongly inclined to think that I was deluded about my man-hating tendencies. And his preference was at least partially responsible for my preference, which was to conceal that part of my character whenever possible, to ignore it, defy it, or minimize it . . . to emphasize instead the side of myself that was gentle, benign, the side that had managed to assimilate the best and the worst of experiences, coming out of them seemingly "whole."

While I was thinking about that, I looked at my friend and saw his face transform into a caricature of itself, into a grotesque. "Stop it," I whispered to myself. "He's only trying to reassure me." But was he trying to reassure me? Or was he trying to reassure himself? Because if I was a man-hater, then who knew how many man-haters were concealed beneath the surface charms of women he liked or regarded as friends? Against this threat to its existence the Man-Hating Creature in me had retaliated, distorting my friend until he was scarcely recognizable . . . for "It" knew, as I was beginning to know, that I could no longer afford to be concerned about reassuring myself *or* him, when what I really needed was to face what I felt, exactly what I felt, whether it was pleasant or not.

"Why is it so hard," I thought. "Why can't I just acknowledge it squarely, show the anxiety and the hostility instead of camouflaging them?"

And I knew that a large part of the reason why I *couldn't* had to do with need: men's need for women, and women's need for men. My need for men prevented me from being as honest as I might have been otherwise . . . need, friendship, and the requirements of love.

All around me I saw ambivalence. Nothing but ambivalence. And I didn't think I had ever loved anyone unambivalently, male or female. Love was capable of making me dependent. Need strengthened that dependency and made me afraid of it. Fear made me hostile. Biological gaps strengthened the hostility. Social gaps set it in concrete. Personal experience created an unbreakable fossil.

What a ubiquitous thing this man-hating was. There might be times when it appeared only in my dreams, and others when it surfaced with peculiar vehemence on behalf of others, when the power of self-identification became so strong that I lost the ability to distinguish myself from someone else. Sometimes it cropped up under completely impersonal circumstances, circumstances that other people were able to ignore more easily than I; sometimes it appeared in the most intimate of situations, when I was with men who were my friends, or men who were my lovers. The range of climates in which it thrived, and the variety of its intensity, could be astounding. It could live through a dry year, cropping up, tougher than ever, after a single summer storm. It seemed, finally, to be all but indestructible.

But indestructible or not, my friend had not even believed that it existed. So I found myself searching for an explanation of what made me a man-hater, or rather, of what a man-hater was.

It wasn't easy. I didn't really know what the qualifications were. Did one have to be a man-hater all the time to fit the category? Or did the mere existence of the category function as a protective barrier against the reality? If one were as capable (or thought oneself as capable) of loving as of hating, did one still "belong"? Wasn't it possible that the word itself was designed to make distinctions which were unrealistic, distinctions that forced women to choose a "side"—the man-hating side having such disagreeable overtones that almost anyone would choose not to be on it?

Wasn't that, after all, what my friend had meant . . . that I wasn't "that kind of woman," wasn't "the man-hating type"? But real man-hating, I thought, unlike its theatrical counterpart, is probably more often concealed than revealed, more often a source of terror than of celebratory exhibitionism, more often an interweaving of multiple unknown forces than an outburst of a single force. Certainly all man-haters could not be depended upon to behave in any particular way. (For myself I knew that my man-hating was admirably resourceful and could always devise new ways in which to express itself.) Probably there were man-haters of all shapes and sizes and styles and symptoms floating around . . . a great many of them fast asleep in the arms of men they love, a great many having dinner with men, going for walks with them, engaging in animated discussions with them. Probably you could scratch a flirt, a liberationist, a housewife, a career woman, a sex goddess, even a contented woman, whatever that is, and find beneath their delicate skins, a great many squirmy little man-hating creatures making their way slowly but persistently through their bloodstreams.

Who knew? It might even turn out that deep down many, or perhaps even *most,* women had a man-hater crouched somewhere inside of them, waiting.

2

I cannot stand to walk down the street and hear men make "psst, psst" noises at me from the sidewalk or from the safety of their cars. I cannot stand riding the subways during the rush hour. Both situations turn me into a man-hater. The "psst, pssts" are bad enough even though the assault is exclusively verbal. But the subways represent the worst threat to command of one's own body that I have ever experienced.

The general circumstances are simple enough: bodies, all of them, are tightly pressed together. A man presses his body to mine. I cannot tell whether it is the general crush that is putting him in that position, whether he is deriving an extra pleasure from the opportunity, whether he is as uncomfortable as I am, or whether he is going to take advantage of the situation to do a little bit of exploring. Whatever his intention, my mind begins to throw off sparks. And the reason is that *so many* men have had hands that turned into veritable demons of research under cover of the ambiguous circumstances, that I am no longer capable of even *trying* to understand the situation. Anticipation alone is enough to make me break out in a cold sweat of absolute terror. My associative thread progresses to one point, and then snaps off. It is the point when I was twelve years old, rode the subway home from school and stood in a frozen panic while a man who was looking straight into my face, managed to lift my skirt with his hidden hand and touch me. I could feel tears blocking my lungs, but I was too ashamed to say anything, so I just tried to squirm away. The hand followed me, and from one moment to the next I could see his face, thoroughly impassive, seeming to concentrate only on the subway poster ads. A woman standing next to me finally noticed my anguished expression. She turned to me and whispered, "Are you all right?" I shook my head no and started to cry. At the next stop she took over the responsibility for rescuing me and, together with a press of furious passengers, shoved the man off the train. By then I was sobbing hysterically, and although the woman tried to comfort me saying, "Well those people are sick, try not to be too upset," I was not to be comforted.

From that time on I became terrified of riding the subways during the rush hour, terrified if a man stood near me. My fear, it seemed, was all too often justified. For between the time I was twelve and the time I was fifteen, such incidents or variations of them—men exposing themselves, men following me down the street, men whispering dirty words in my ear, men staring at me until I shrank away—happened repeatedly. Once, on the subway during the rush hour, my anger outstripped my fear, and I ground the metal spike of a new pair of high-heel shoes into the foot of the molester. When his face crunched up with pain, I was gratified, and the gratification concealed for a moment the awful visions of violation which more and more often crowded my mind, so that even an "ordinary" subway ride or excursion provoked, at the very least, a frantic bout with the specters of my imagination.

Gradually, my fear magnified into hatred. And I became permanently paralyzed into expecting the worst. Since the worst often happened, this was not a totally paranoid delusion.

Unfortunately, however, even though it was only one man at a time who was responsible for "bothering" me, my own patterns of hatred developed so that sometimes they extended to every man on the subway, including and sometimes especially, the friendly ones who smiled at me over the tops of the offenders' heads, as well as the oblivious ones quietly absorbed in reading their newspapers. For those men could afford to ride the subways and be friendly or oblivious. The subway crush for them might be a problem of overcrowding of the city's transportation facilities, a problem of being pushed and shoved unpleasantly, a problem perhaps of feeling alienated from a sea of anonymous beings, or even a problem of unbearable claustrophobia. But for me, it was always all of those things plus sheer terror and attacks of man-hating which made me limp with nausea.

I am sure that not everyone who had similar experiences was affected in the same way. Certainly those situations are common enough. The victims, more often than not, are young girls, who are not used to the sight of a man with an erection, not used to being touched sexually. In my case, partly because I was easily stimulated sexually, the assaults represented a double threat. Perhaps also because I was in general sensitive to all kinds of experiences, such violations left a deeper mark on me than they did on other girls. In any case, the result was devastating.

There were times, even during my adult life, when a repetition of such experiences, or even the *memory* of them, was enough for me to vent my anger and disgust on every nice man of my acquaintance by being bitchy or paranoid; times when I would walk outside the subway, head for the nearest toilet and throw up; times when I might, as I did at the age of twelve, simply *endure,* trying to twist inconspicuously away, meanwhile noticing with a mixture of horror and bewilderment that those men didn't look any different from anyone else, that in fact they usually looked nice enough and couldn't be told apart from Mr. Jones who ran the grocery store. The result of the fact that they were not "marked" in any way, made me suspect every other similarly "unmarked" male of possibly possessing the same kind of inclinations in varying forms. So I grew up mistrusting "nice men" as much as those men who did, in fact, try to molest me, grew up imagining that anyone who came within a foot of me was about to attack me, grew up feeling, alongside of my positive sexual drive, recurrent surges of disgust toward all forms of sexuality whatsoever.

. . .

A similar kind of impersonal hatred crops up in me whenever I hitchhike and am picked up by someone who, for as long as I am with him, considers my body to be his possession. A few years ago while I was traveling out to California, a truckdriver picked me up and before five minutes were over, he had pulled over to a truck stop.

"Wanna climb in back?" he asked.

"No thanks," I said politely, having gotten used to this sort of thing, even though I could feel the hatred trying to climb around my politeness.

"Whaddya mean, no thanks?"

"Look mister, I told you when I got in that I just wanted a ride. I have my dog with me for protection. What do you think that means?"

"I dunno," he said. "How do you expect to get across the country if you ain't willing to do it? Just takes a few minutes, that's all."

"How do boys get across the country?"

"You ain't a boy. And girls is different."

"Well I'm not different. At least not in that respect. And all I want is to get to where I'm going."

"You will, if you're gonna pay your way. Otherwise, forget it."

"Then I'll just have to forget it, won't I?" And I climbed out of the cab dragging my knapsack behind me, thinking that I was going to have to walk all the way back to the highway, thinking of the last time that had happened, while I was hitching from Cambridge to Boston. Then, the fellow had been less ceremonious. He had simply grabbed my breast and pulled me toward him, after swerving off the main road into an abandoned lot. Some long-repressed rage swelled up inside of me and while he was pulling at me I fired my elbow into his belly and yelled, with my head just inches from its destination, "If you don't let go of me, I swear I'll bit your cock off." I suppose that startled him because he let go and said, "OK, OK lady. You don't have to get so wild about it"—at which point I simply jumped out of the car, surprised by my own outburst and freshly pleased that at last I'd been able to retaliate.

This joy in retaliation became such a force in my life that from time to time I actually looked forward to situations in which I would be free to express it, since the daily accumulation of petty hatred rarely found such direct outlets. (Which certainly does not speak well for my own mental equilibrium and says only that distortion is capable of producing more distortion.)

In any case, these vignettes have a third point to make, beyond the obvious ones of men's vulgarization of women, and women's (my) crippled responses. This point is that my hostility at such times extended to an enormous number of innocents . . . to all the boys who made it across the country "free" (both literally and figuratively), even though boys *do* run the similar hazard of being propositioned by homosexuals. For boys, however, that may be the only chance they get to understand what it's like to be a woman on the road, or even walking down the street, the chief difference being that men boast about their actions in relation to women and take it for granted that such approaches are natural, whereas homosexuals are usually more covert about it. The other people my hatred swept up were the men who would say in response to all this, "Well, girls shouldn't hitchhike in the first place, just because things like this *do* happen." That's like saying women shouldn't be free because men are unreliable or crude or "bad" . . . a fine rationalization for the status quo.

Similar, though less dramatic situations, occur almost daily, whether one is adventurous or not. They occur every time a woman decides to go for a walk around New York at night, even on Fifth Avenue, and even if—as in my case—the woman has no fear of being mugged. But every time I want to walk, I have to take into consideration that my desire to be alone won't be acknowledged by the men who haunt the streets, that if I want to think, I'd better do my thinking at home, that if I need some air, I'd better stretch my head out the window.

Such problems occur, in short, every time a woman decides to do *something* alone, whether it is going for a walk or sitting in a bar or restaurant or taking a trip to the beach. Whereas there is nothing at all extraordinary about a man alone, a woman alone is often thought of as somehow incomplete, so that seeking a secluded corner of a beach means that someone will follow you, and you will be safer sitting in the public section; sitting at a bar, even if you just want to watch what's going on or do some thinking over a glass of something or other, means that you are waiting to be picked up, and if you walk down the street alone at night, your solitude implies to many men that you are sexually available.

For those of us who are loners by nature and conviction, such prohibitions can and do take on staggering proportions, severely limiting our freedom of movement as well as our psychic freedom to the point that one's own character becomes an oppressive liability. For myself, not being inclined to passivity in such situations, I brave the consequences. And end up hating.

There are, of course, circumstances in which the whole business is handled with a good deal more finesse. "Favors" are the perfect example. Being a woman earns you "favors" at a price. If I'm friendly to the mechanic who is working on my car, he offers to do the work faster, to deliver the car in person and to screw me for the same price. The same goes for the man at the grocery store who offers free delivery and, when he arrives, stands grinning suggestively in front of my door until I insist that he leave . . . the delicatessen man whose conversation is an intricate network of sexual innuendo . . . the cop who won't give you a ticket, if instead of expressing your fury over the fact that you didn't deserve it, you flirt with him for a while or else cry . . . the photographer who offers to do your portrait since you have such an "interesting and unusual" face, and then turns out not to possess even a camera—let alone a darkroom—and his "studio" is fully occupied by a double bed.

Personally, I've reached the point where I regard friendliness toward most people of the opposite sex as a very risky business, and no longer accept favors from anyone, since I can't tell the difference between those that are meant well and those that have strings attached (often the offers with the most strings are made by men who are the quickest to say "no strings attached").

The last time I accepted such a favor, somewhat against my better judgment, was in Mexico. I had been sitting in a newly opened restaurant for an hour talking with the owner, since I was the only customer. He was fascinated with the hippies and articulated in English how meaningful it was to reject materialistic values in search of spiritual ones, how Mexico had not yet reached that stage of development, how it was difficult for poor people to understand why anyone would choose poverty, how he hoped that such a renascence of spiritual values would ultimately transform the entire world.

When I was finished eating and asked for the bill, he said, "No, no. For friendship and understanding. You are a young writer. I understand you have not much money. The next time. Come whenever you like. I am happy to meet you." I said that I appreciated the offer, but would still like to pay. He insisted that he would take no money from me. So I thanked him and accepted, thinking of all the stories I'd heard about Mexican generosity, about Zorba the Greek, and assorted other characters of various nationalities who made young travelers feel a sense of warmth and camaraderie.

Then I left the restaurant and started walking back to my hotel. Within minutes I heard a voice behind me. It was the restaurant owner. "Here we go again," I thought. And sure enough, he wanted me to come and stay with him. When I said I already had a hotel, he insisted it didn't matter: I should leave the hotel and stay free at his place.

I still refused, refused adamantly (glad that for the moment at least I had enough money not to be dependent on anyone's offers) and finally began to walk away when he seemed unwilling to accept my refusal. While I was walking, he shouted after me, "So why do you think I fed you? Do you think people get meals for free here?"

I turned around and said, "Look, I didn't ask you for anything. You offered. But if you tell me what the bill was, I'll pay you right now."

"No, no," he said. "You don't have to pay. I don't want you to pay. Come with me. For just this night, you understand."

"I don't want to come. I want to pay the bill and go home. So tell me what I owe you."

"Fifteen pesos," he said, his face growing sour.

I knew it was too much, since all I'd eaten was a bowl of fish soup, but I wasn't about to argue. I held out a hundred peso bill. "Do you have change?" I asked.

"No," he said.

"Well that's all I have with me."

"Can we make a deal then?"

"No, no deals. Is there any place open where I could get change?"

"No, nothing open."

"Well, then tomorrow. I'll bring you the money tomorrow," I said. "Is that all right?"

He nodded sullenly and made one last try. "You sure you not come with me?" he asked.

"Yes I'm sure. I'll pay you tomorrow. Goodnight."

I turned and walked back to the hotel, feeling the hatred rising up inside of me like some cold, smothering force, which suddenly extended to all of the boys I'd known who had "charming experiences" with the Mexicans.

The next day I "forgot" to go back to the restaurant. I had a lot of things to do and planned to leave for a tiny village by boat at ten in the morning. Maybe that was the only way I had of paying him back. Maybe it gave him an excuse to hate women for "taking advantage" of his generosity. I don't know and I don't care. I might have gained a moral victory if I had "remembered," as I insisted to myself the night before I would, to return the money. But a moral victory seemed cheap at that point. What I wanted was revenge. I thought the one I'd chosen was mild enough, all things considered.

During the same trip to Mexico, I encountered another occasion for man-hating. Three young, long-haired musicians offered to let me sleep at the house where they were staying. Unfortunately, at that point I still tended to think of young longhairs as being different from other men, and knew that crashing was as common as cornflakes. Besides, the house belonged to a family, an American psychologist and his sculptor wife. Certainly respectable enough.

So I accepted the invitation gladly, all the more so since I was running low on funds. Five of us—the three boys, the son of the Americans and I—all slept in the same room in sleeping bags on the floor, surrounded by books with high-minded titles which ran the gamut from Proust and

Faulkner to Marxist philosophy, neo-Freudian investigation, and contemporary sociological analysis.

During the night I dreamed that I was in the middle of having an orgasm. I woke to find that I was partially out of my unzipped sleeping bag, that my nightgown was up around my waist, that one of the boys was quietly though insistently touching me and that I was in fact on the verge of having an orgasm. I groaned and flipped over on my stomach, burning with embarrassment for having responded to such an impersonal touch. At first I thought that maybe I had dreamed the whole thing, but I tried to stay awake long enough so I would be sure. After half an hour I was positive. And after half an hour the hatred had built up inside of me so much that I not only hated the boy but also hated myself because I was sexually responsive when I chose not to be.

So what should I have done in that case? Jumped up and yelled? Slit the boy's throat? Taken him to court? Slugged him? Walked out on the street in the middle of the night (where most assuredly I would be accosted)?

I couldn't bring myself to do any of those things, and for a moment I had a glimpse into the emotional condition of a woman who has been raped. On the one hand, my body bore no signs of assault (many rapes, I'm well aware, don't even involve any bruises). I was, physically, totally intact. The damage was strictly emotional, and not only that, but in the midst of it, I had had an ambivalent response which made me feel guilty, although in fact I had no direct responsibility for anything. If I kept silent I was being masochistic . . . if I made a fuss I would feel humiliated. And no act of aggression that I could envision would have taken care of what I felt. For invariably when one reacts with a great deal of emotion to such individual and isolated incidents, the reactions seem out of proportion to the offense and take on the quality of hysterical outbursts. A convenient sort of double bind for those of us who are struggling with the idea of emancipation: if you do nothing you're masochistic and if you do *something,* you're hysterical, since the cumulative weight of the events is almost never taken into consideration.

In the grip of such contradictions, I retreated and became passive. Morning came and I found myself incapable of looking the boy straight in the eye, especially since he was dressed in a pair of immaculate white pants and an immaculate white jersey, and appeared to be so pure, so innocent that it was almost easier to doubt myself than to doubt him.

When the family came in for breakfast, I told them I was leaving. I gave no explanation. They seemed surprised but asked no questions.

After breakfast, the father, whom I had met only the night before in a brief introduction, said to me, "Guess my son didn't give you a good fuck, eh?"

My body suddenly went rigid.

"Oh, don't think I care," he said. "I don't care who he fucks. I don't care if you fucked all four of them."

I picked up my things and started to walk out the door.

"Hey look, don't be insulted," the father called out after me. "I didn't mean to offend you."

I said nothing and just kept walking.

"All right," he said, following me. "Maybe you didn't do it with any of them."

"Look," I said, trying not to break. "I'm leaving because I want to be alone. That's all. I just want to be alone."

"You mean you don't *like* sleeping in a room with four boys?" he asked.

"I like being alone when I want to be alone."

"Oh I see," he said. "Well I'm sorry . . . I didn't mean . . . I mean I didn't realize . . . none of them bothered you, did they?"

In an instant I'd been transformed from whore to angel, from someone the father might take on himself to an innocent in need of paternal protection. What else is there?

I was unable to look at him. "No, they didn't bother me," I said.

"Well that's good. At least . . ." his voice trailed off. "Listen," he finally said. "I know a woman . . . she lives alone . . . her son and her daughter are away. She's a very good person. I'm sure she would put you up for a few nights. You'd have peace and quiet and no one would get in your way."

"No thanks, I'll stay in a hotel." (I didn't know *which* hotel since the two I could afford were filled.)

"Look," he said. "I'm really sorry. I just didn't understand. I mean it, she's a very nice woman. I could walk you over there, and if you don't like her you don't have to stay. At least I can do that much . . ."

I felt so battered at that point that I didn't much care what happened any more. Perhaps I had also reached the stage where one is grateful for *any* help, even if it comes on the heels of an insult. So I went with him to his friend's house; she really *was* a very nice woman, and I finally stayed there. She could have been a relative, someone whose name might have been included on a list of addresses my family would have given me, someone whom ordinarily I would have avoided, since middle class anxiety and protectiveness were anathema to me. But suddenly she seemed to me to be the epitome of health, maturity, and stability. I was quite content to spend my time with her, doing no more than talk about the trials and tribulations of a divorced, liberal-intellectual mother, who had been in analysis, had a son with a drug problem, considered herself averagely neurotic, and wasn't quite sure what to do with her life. She was familiar terrain, safe, sturdy in her own way, and very comforting.

For a week I was in revolt against bohemian living, modern anthropology and sociology, Mexican longhairs, colorful expatriates, and the Left. When I jumped overboard, I left nothing behind, not bothering to separate the real object of my hatred from the things that had surrounded it. All I wanted now was my books, my solitude, and Molly for company. I imagined that I might even take up knitting and get into the habit of going to bed at ten o'clock. I imagined that my hatred of men had reached such an advanced stage that it was no longer conceivable to have anything but "cordial" relations with them.

Certainly every time I went down to the square and saw my ex-companions strolling around, I managed to be coolly polite. They were also polite. And after a while I was able to look at the offender and evaluate how nice he looked without thinking that a piece of shrapnel from my anger was going to fly straight into his brown clear eyes. By then the hatred had come to rest inside of me, pure, solid, and hard as rock. Quite detached, I could judge him nice-looking.

After a week, the travel bug was at me again. The security and comfort of Molly's place were no longer quite so soothing. And besides, deep down I knew that the town had been spoiled for me after that night—Molly's "normality" notwithstanding. My hatred had contaminated everything. I had no desire to come back.

So I hit the road, though for another week, at least once a day, the question entered my mind: What did I do to provoke that? And how was I responsible?

There was only one logical answer. I was responsible because I put myself in a position where those kinds of things *could* happen. If I voluntarily curtailed my freedom, if I stopped taking risks, if I stopped accepting friendly invitations altogether, stopped talking to strangers (but on a trip in a foreign country, isn't *everyone* a stranger?), stopped traveling alone—in short, if I shifted the focus of my attention from adventure and exploration to simple, straight tourism, if I stopped looking for interesting peasant families and interesting circumstances (the old man who carved figures in a dark corner, hidden from anyone but the most industrious explorer . . . the little workers' restaurants concealed in out of the way corners of the city . . . the remote villages of the jungle, accessible only on horseback . . .) then I would be safe—or at least safer. But doing that would make me miserable. It would give me a boring, standardized trip. It would mean following the same route everyone took, the route of passing through and brushing elbows with the locals only when they ran the hotel you lived in or sold you a piece of pineapple in the *mercado.* It would mean cutting myself off from every spontaneous situation, and giving in to the idea that men could have all sorts of fascinating experiences that were closed to me as a woman.

The conclusion I came to was that I was "responsible" in the same sense that slaves are responsible for being beaten if they refuse to act like slaves. I had chosen to be "emancipated" and was paying the price. Wasn't it the same price I had been paying for years?

Still, I had to acknowledge that there was psychological truth to the idea that anyone who is repeatedly abused in one form or another learns to *expect* it, to feel vaguely that if something hasn't happened yet, then it will the following day, and to derive an almost relieved pleasure when it does happen (now I don't have to worry about it happening tomorrow). There does seem to be only a quota of misery that human beings can tolerate without adapting themselves to their circumstances and learning to take a perverse pleasure in their misfortune ("see I told you so") . . . even sometimes seeking it out. The truth of the matter is that I have become so accustomed to such incidents that I would think something was wrong if they didn't take place.

So the pattern, it seems, congealed in me. I *expected* to

get into difficult situations. And I got into difficult situations. Which came first, the chicken or the egg? . . . the sociological or the psychological? Whichever came first, it was clear that the two forces were mutually supportive: an environment that made it hazardous for me to live anything but a sheltered life, and a growing masochistic adaptation to that environment. Masochism, too, it seemed, was one of the costs I had to add to the price of female existence.

Although the surcharge, of course, was hatred.

So far there has probably been very little for the average man to associate himself with. If I were to stop the chapter right here, anyone reading it would probably agree with my friend that I'm not a man-hater, that I'm just angry when I have a perfectly good reason to be angry. And that would be the truth, because in everything I've recounted so far, there has been a visible chain of cause and effect. My man-hating has taken a relatively innocuous form related strictly to circumstance. My responses have not been very much out of proportion to the provocations. If anything, they have not been aggressive or hostile enough, all things considered.

But is that all? Is that really the end of it? Or is it just the beginning, since the circumstances I've described have been just that—impersonal circumstances? My hatred was aroused by men I didn't really know and who didn't know me, men who just happened to be crude or cruel or preying or perverted. And because of that impersonality, it was sometimes possible for me to incorporate or even dismiss the experiences.

What I really had to come to terms with, though, was something else, or rather someone else. It was the average guy himself, the men I didn't know but who were nonetheless part of my daily life, the men who moved across my perceptual screen as representing "the kind of man I'm drawn to," or "the kind of man I would like to know better," the men who at one time or another I had thought might make good platonic friends.

Until now, my negative reactions to them had been mostly extensions of reactions to experiences that had nothing to do with them, my responses widening out to include all men, individual incidents reverberating until every male was affected.

But not all my attacks of man-hating derived from such impersonal circumstances. After all, it should have been relatively easy to dispose of the impersonal situations, and to gain strength from the average male. But the fact of the matter was that even though any decent man would divorce himself from such brutalities, would say that he could never do such a thing, I still had attacks of man-hating which were directed toward the average guy as well, attacks which sometimes became most virulent toward precisely those men who were the most understanding on the surface, the most tolerant and the least deserving of hatred.

I knew that those men were the ones I really had to come to terms with. And knew, too, that from here on the situation would become more subtle, more ambiguous, and more confusing, that I would have to deal not only with men as agents, society as solidifier, but in the long run, with *myself,* with things that had gone off the track and were rusting in the junkyard of my spirit, bones as well as fragments of mind and flesh, which I'd tried unsuccessfully to destroy, or else to bury.

3

It is a warm spring day. I am sitting in a restaurant across the table from an editor who has expressed an interest in my work. He has just ordered something elegant and unpronounceable, and the *maître d'*, who seems to have taken me on as his personal responsibility, leans toward me to ask, *"Tout va bien, madame?"* Five minutes later he comes back to make sure that I am satisfied, even though there is still nothing on my plate but a napkin.

The editor and I are having a friendly conversation. He thinks I might like to write a book for his publishing house.

"What is impressive about your writing," he says, "is its authenticity and the fact that, even though you are angry, you seem to be free from bitterness. There isn't any emotional damage, if you see what I mean."

A few warning sparks go off. It occurs to me that I must be even more camouflaged than I suspected. "Emotional damage," after all, is not something one bandages up or puts in a splint. It has the doubtful advantage of not being immediately apparent to the general public. (If it *is* apparent, one checks into the nearest hospital or cries at home alone or chokes out the explanatory words in a parenthetically enclosed analytic session.)

"Yes, I see what you mean," I say smiling. (One of these days I'm going to put bandaids across my mouth so that smiling will become less of a reflex in uncomfortable situations.)

At the very instant that I start smiling, an image flashes through my mind of the construction workers I had passed on my way to the restaurant. They did their usual number, and I surprised myself by being surprised. Not only was I surprised, but I reacted more intensely than I ever had before, reacted so intensely that it shocked even me. I gave them the finger and had a fantasy about ramming that finger (a weapon and phallic substitute) up the most well-shaped ass around, ramming it so hard that the man would fly right up the scaffolding. In my other hand was a cigarette, and after *that* particular vision had worn itself out, my imagination came up with a new torture; I felt a powerful desire to walk back to the site and stab the burning coal into whatever eye ("if thine eye offend me . . .") happened to be most available. I considered aiming for the genitals, but so far, even in my fantasies (though not my dreams), I cringed before the crunch. Besides, I do not look forward to living in a nation of eunuchs, and would basically much prefer to have men around with all of their parts intact, though not quite so enslaved to the indiscriminate exercise of those parts.

I wanted to be calm for the meeting with the editor, though, so I tried to push the incident and the fantasies out of my mind. But instead I found myself remembering another incident that had taken place a year before. It was in the form of a dream I had while driving my car out to California. I was traveling with two boys, one of whom was very upset over the fact that I seemed able to handle everything, which certainly was not true. In order to soothe his ego, I had made an effort to restrain myself from offering too many suggestions or making too many decisions. The effort had yielded no results (perhaps because I was so ambivalent that I never really surrendered without making it clear what I was doing).

One afternoon while I was asleep in the back seat of the car, I had a dream: I was listening to the radio and heard the announcer say that a horrible crime had just been committed . . . a man had been murdered and tortured, his genitals chewed to bits, as if by a rat. I listened to the broadcast and was terrified. The announcer added that the criminal had not yet been intercepted, whereupon I broke into a sweat. I shut off the radio and put my hands over my ears.

At that point I woke up. And looked at the boys sitting in the front seat. What had they done? I thought. What kind of a monster was I? Did I really want to castrate men? Murder and torture them? Should I warn every man I met that he was dealing with dynamite? Or should I take the attitude that dreams like that were normal?

Certianly they didn't seem normal to me. Nor did my reaction to the construction workers seem normal, especially since it was a common enough sort of encounter and since I had already talked and written about my reactions.

Looking at the editor and thinking of his comment on "emotional damage," I wondered whether I should tell him about all *that;* about boys and dreams and construction workers? I couldn't do it, so I remained silent. But I felt as if I had been put into a tiny room alone with my self-image. The two of us were going to have to battle things out. For on the one hand there was the tolerant, rational "me," who regarded men as human and therefore flawed . . . just like myself. On the other hand there was this fierce, unacknowledged "me," who supplied facts to fit my preconceptions of truth, who lashed out irrationally, who spoke to me through my dreams . . . a me who hated and could always find good reasons for hating.

Trying to understand this "me" had recently brought me face to face with a whole set of real, though nonetheless unfulfillable, expectations—which I had tried to repress in the interests of fairness. Most of those expectations hinged around the idea of change. They consisted largely of an unspoken belief that talking about the need for change was the same thing as changing things . . . the belief that once I expressed annoyance or hostility about something, that would be enough to alter it. If I was bothered by construction workers and handle-with-care male egos, then all I had to do was *say so* and presto! construction workers would start giving me friendly smiles, travel companions would stop feeling threatened, dreams already dissected would be freed from the elements they contained. On the larger scale I expected that discussing what it was like to be a woman together with a man would instantly close the psychic gap between us. In short, I believed that the articulation of rage would transform the sources of rage . . . that the present would go skittering into the future unencumbered by the past. Now, with the editor, I wasn't so sure. For I had already seen such attempts fail, over and over and over again. And knew that when words as artifacts of communication had no visible effect on either myself (on my own capacities to deal with things) or on the world around me, frustration was added to anger, creating a network of hostility so dense and so complex that its original source seemed to vanish in a suffocating tangle of exaggerated responses. Until rage and hatred blocked out every other reaction to experience, now preceding the situations that had once been necessary to provoke them. Until I forgot completely that changes in myself had always taken years to effect.

I realized suddenly that my castration fantasy might just as easily have applied to the editor, and that my first early sparks of hostility had to do with the fact that indirectly I held the editor and all the other men who could walk out a door and think only about getting from one place to another or at least think about whatever was going on *inside* their heads . . . held them all responsible for the construction workers and even held them responsible for the tangle of emotions that I felt in relation to the construction workers . . . the indignation mixed with a spiteful sort of pleasure, the pride mixed with humiliation.

Somewhere inside of me I believed that if men could only provide alternative sources of *real* pride, could respond with some sort of clear-cut decency to me as a woman, then I wouldn't have to fight so hard against this

"thing" which I found degrading and which
theless dependent upon.

Of course I was proud to be a woman . . .
of a subtle kind of sexuality. But I was not proud of the way
in which that sexuality was systematically abused in the service of something that ultimately cheapened both me and it.

I held the editor and other "average guys" responsible for such things because they seemed to lack the courage to "betray their sex" by repudiating the attitudes of the construction workers (except in conversations with women, where words are often cheap) *and* lacked the courage to defend women or supply alternatives within their own spheres of influence which would provide a different kind of pride to those women whose egos badly needed it . . . and not only from our own sex.

The area where the editor had influence was in the world of publishing. And he was willing, of course, to publish books written by angry young women, especially if they might be regarded by his publishing house as potentially profitable. What he was less likely to do, however, was take a stand on aspects of the issue that were riskier and more personal.

One such aspect involved me directly. It also had to do with publishing . . . specifically, with book contracts. Although when I was having lunch with the editor, I knew nothing about such contracts, my later exposure to them added retroactive fuel to my anger.

Literary contracts, it seems, are all phrased in the masculine gender. At the beginning of the contract that I signed for this book, for example, I found the following phrase: "The Author, hereinafter referred to in the masculine singular . . ." And in each reference to "The Author" which followed, "she"—in this case me—was designated as "he."

It was not just a question of those built-in linguistic confusions (history-herstory, mankind-womankind) which feminists have long objected to, but more directly a question of self-identification.

Concerned as writers must be with the use and abuse of words, being called "he" when you are "she" is a blatant violation of one's sense of self. On the one hand, of course, female authors, including myself, are proud of authorial accomplishments. One dislikes making an exaggerated commotion, especially since according to publishing houses and editors, the phrasing of contracts is a convention, no more, no less. On the other hand, such conventions, multiplied a thousand times over, are what make daily life such a morass of petty nonrecognitions and ambivalent situations—raising us up on one side while pushing us down on the other—that one feels obliged to take a stand on even the pettiest of issues.

Contracts that substitute "he" for "she" invariably provoke a split reaction, just as the attentions of construction workers provoke split reactions. And construction workers, even if they are not specifically conscious of the fact that women have such few sources of authentic, individual pride that we react ambivalently to whatever "offerings" are made to us, *are* conscious that their heckling and provocations bring on not only a frown of anger, but sometimes a half-smile as well.

In both cases, there is a hidden assumption that women's pride and pleasure (whether in their bodies or their minds) will outweigh their hostility. Of course, writing is more important to me than my body, so that in the case of the contract, my pride and pleasure did outweigh my hostility, whereas in the case of the construction workers my hostility outweighed my pride and pleasure. But that was because I was not so dependent on the construction workers. My life did not revolve around my sexual attractiveness, and if no construction workers ever looked at me again, I wouldn't feel any sense of loss. Five years ago, however, when I believed that my primary worth for men had to do with being physically seductive, I too felt ambivalent about construction workers, and even dressed to provoke the kinds of reactions that I, at bottom, detested. Why not? I wanted attention, and that was the only kind of attention I was able to get. I am sure that for women who spend their days doing mediocre work, or women who feel that they are not attractive enough to gain the interest of men on a basis which is more gratifying to them, the verbal advances of construction workers, even if they are extremely crude, will never be easy to reject . . . unless, of course, they can get attention for other, more important things.

The parallel between construction workers and editors or publishing houses becomes more apparent when seen in this context. On the intellectual scale, contracts that substitute "he" for "she" set up the same bind for a woman desirous of serious attention as do the voices of construction workers calling a woman a cunt when she wants to be acknowledged as a person. The first, of course, is far less blatant and less directly insulting. But it is nonetheless disturbing.

I thought about the contract problem for a full week before requesting a change. I was told that the contract could be altered, but that the editor's secretary, who I know has better things to do with her time, would have to retype the entire thing, substituting "she" wherever "he" appeared. The choice was between creating extra work for a secretary or backing down on the request. I backed down—and was left with the uncomfortable awareness that every woman who objected to the phrasing of a contract would be forced to make herself an exception, forced to make a fuss over something that ought to be assumed.

Most people, of course, would say that the contract issue in itself is very small, that what really counts is having the contract in the first place and being able to do what I want to do. Most people would also say that the issue of the construction workers is very small. What matters they would say, is the way you see *yourself.* Which is certainly true. But the way I see myself is subtly affected by the cumulative presence of situations that put various kinds of pressure on me.

There are a great many women, I am sure, who have learned to ignore construction workers as well as the minor indignities (the "male ego" presumption of their employers, for example) of daily living. But in order to ignore those things, they must anesthetize themselves to feelings which are real and painful. It was something I couldn't do.

Nor was I able to ignore the fact that when my encounter with the construction workers took place a scant two blocks from where I was to meet the editor, not a single man in the crowd had batted an eyelash. They all found it simpler to pay no attention.

I could not help thinking that every time I heard whites make even unconsciously disparaging remarks about blacks, I at least said something that made it clear which side I was on. I could not replace the efforts blacks must make on their own behalf. I *could,* however, supplement those efforts. Just as men can supplement the efforts of women . . . not in theoretical discussions about women's liberation at the dinner table, but in the specific situations that occur unexpectedly every day and require responses.

It isn't necessary to start a brawl in the middle of Fifth Avenue. Nor is it necessary to "protect a lady in distress." (Ideally, everyone should be expected to protect everyone else, male or female, in distress.) What's necessary is to take a stand on behalf of humane behavior, even if such stands produce no immediate effect. (The citizens of the Warsaw ghetto, for example, may have waged a hopeless battle against the Nazis, but the battle in itself confirmed them as human beings determined to maintain their self-respect at all costs.) Human indignity, as far as I can tell, is something to be consciously resisted on every scale, from the smallest to the largest. Just as I am responsible for myself, as a female and a human being, I consider men to be responsible for themselves in precisely the same ways. Not responsible for giving lectures or distributing pamphlets or tangling with construction workers or washing dishes better than I (not a difficult task to fulfill), but simply for demonstrating at those moments when it is inconvenient to do so, that sympathy is not the easily peeled rind of their being.

Unfortunately though, most men were so thoroughly implicated *themselves* in the attitudes underlying the comments of construction workers (without having their lively verve) that they usually didn't even notice anything unusual about them, let alone object. Moreover, once a construction worker has singled out a particular "body," they will usually join in the ogling . . . except more covertly. Which is not the very worst thing a man can do. The worst comes later when precisely these same men express their affinity with the deepest aims of women, demonstrating that well-nigh intolerable though highly common male trait: an inability to tell women the truth. In general, when it comes to the domain of feeling, to acknowledging the consequences of one's own actions and perceptions to a woman, a man would much rather lie than tell the truth, which, even if it causes a great deal of initial pain, is the only way to get from A to B. Most every man would rather tell a woman, *any* woman, that he is for women's rights, than admit to the welter of contradictory feelings he has in relation to women and construction workers; because it is always easier to go along with a woman (even if you don't) than provoke the kind of emotional response—whether tears or polemics—which men expect from a woman. What is easiest of all for a man is to be charming and flattering and supportive while not really meaning it. It is even easier since that is the role men are expected to play with women and have traditionally played. And because of the ease of it, because of the similarity it bears to an eager salesman charming a customer into a major deal, I am mistrustful.

I thought I could be reasonably sure that in some hidden part of themselves most men maintained a sense of covert fraternity with oglers. If so, why couldn't they be frank about it and take things from there? Why did respectable men edge up to me surreptitiously instead of staring openly? Was the first more polite even though it was just as obvious? If they could see me, could *watch* me, didn't they assume that I could watch them too? Or was I supposed to be myopic as a goldfish in an aquarium? If men really thought that way, if they had reflexes that came from their glands, just as I had reflexes, why couldn't they simply acknowledge those reflexes without glorifying them or denigrating them? Why did they insist on wearing such a veneer of courtly respectability? How much of themselves had they invested in this conspiracy to conceal their own failings . . . to cover over their bad moves the way they might cover over a poor business deal?

If men were really men, I thought, then they would be willing to take responsibility for their actions and reactions. They would be willing to confront themselves as people instead of as godlike images. They would be able to look at a woman on the street with a clear, wholesome expression, sexually appreciative but not predatory.

For several years I was a notoriously easy pick-up. I hardly ever met anyone *except* on the street. And I know from that period of my life that there are ways of looking at a woman that are warm and friendly, ways in which a woman can respond in kind. Even now it happens every once in a while. Sometimes when I am walking down the street or in the park, a small spark of communication is exchanged, and not pursued, which is exactly the way it should be, since it acknowledges my existence while respecting my privacy.

I thought again of my castration fantasy, of the slaughtered masses that my imagination had laid out on the streets of Fifth Avenue as sacrifices to my fury. Then I looked at the editor. Surely he had his problems . . . surely he too felt lost at times in this profound sexual wilderness or under this dome of distortion. But if I were to tell him about the fantasy, his eyes would probably flicker for a second. Then he would regain his equilibrium and say, "It's a shame women have to undergo . . ." What he would not do, most probably, was admit that with some part of himself he felt a subtle sense of affinity with those workers (even if he might feel it in no other situation), for if such brawny fellows could be the objects of a female rampage, then who could imagine what would happen to men like himself who, on the surface at least, were far more vulnerable to attack. What he would not do was say that, for a split second, he might even have felt an empathetic crunch in the groin on behalf of the construction workers—before separating himself from his emotions enough to understand and sympathize with my position. And yet if he were capable of *admitting* to such feelings, I would respect him much more as a human being struggling for his own identity, than I would if he pretended to go along with things that, in fact, were threatening to him.

I kept thinking how difficult and necessary true communication was, thinking how easily it was subverted by dogmatic beliefs in what communication *ought* to consist of. Most liberal men believed it was right to go along with the basic tenets of women's liberation. But they were not willing to examine with genuine candor what their underlying reactions to those basic tenets were. Once again, their masculine images were at stake, only now that image no longer depended upon taking the "masculine role" of chest-thumping hero, but depended instead on something that was only a variation—a strong and stoical acceptance of what women were asking for. Fundamentally, this doesn't represent anything new. It does not represent the one thing that is absolutely necessary to the struggle for self-liberation: a confrontation with what is real and personal.

Certainly I thought that men hated women as much as women hated men. Certainly I thought that their hatred was equally justified, and considered it valid for a man to say, "Listen, I hate women because women are just as cruel to men as men are to women." I considered *any-*

thing valid that was an expression of genuine feeling, an expression of honest experience. But there, precisely, was where men failed. Because they would rather lie, would rather do anything, than admit to what they genuinely feel . . . would rather flatter, seduce, cajole, or humor a woman than admit to hostility and its ever-present companion, fear.

I thought of the first time I had gotten stoned on pot. I was out on a boat in the middle of a lake. I looked at the sky and the mountains, and was suddenly struck by how closely they resembled men and women in the physical and metaphysical sense, seeming at first glance to touch each other, to communicate on the most intimate scale. Yet everyone knows that in fact sky and mountains don't really touch each other, knows that they exist in very separate spheres. It was only in the story of Chicken Little that the sky was falling. Did the sky then have to fall before men and mountains could meet?

Even though the problem took a concrete visual form for me when I was stoned, the ideas behind the vision remained with me afterward. It seemed to me that the real trouble was that both men and women were surrounded by a thin, almost impenetrable psychic membrane defined by gender. Getting beyond it was an enormous task, but it had to be done if hatred and mistrust were to be overcome.

Of course the attempt to bridge gaps between people through communication and to pierce the barrier of psychic separatism is what we all are concerned with. That is what art, politics (in its current framework), and religion all try to do. That is what people as individuals are trying to do.

I found myself thinking of the esthetic attempts that had been made in that direction . . . of the consequences that resulted from the failures of those attempts. Van Gogh articulated the magnitude of his struggle in each of his paintings, paintings which were, among other things, an effort to exorcise his fantasies, to reach beyond his isolation and affirm a liberated creativity. His efforts never entirely succeeded though and he ended by committing suicide shortly after painting a strangely wild and lost picture of crows streaking across a field which dodged and blazed beneath them. Sylvia Plath wrote *The Bell Jar* as an act of catharsis, for the purpose of disposing of a period of her own life which had been filled with personal disintegration. She managed to recover, but years later, after completing *Ariel,* she put her head in the oven and died. And thousands of more "ordinary" people, who have no direct connection with the creation of art, take part in the same struggle, talking fairly rationally about their problems and the problems of society until one day those problems become larger than they are and they simply, quietly, crack.

For me, the form through which that struggle expresses itself is language, words. The attempt to break through the barriers between men and women with words is both a personal and an esthetic passion. For me words still possess their primitive, mystical, incantatory healing powers. I am inclined to use them as part of an attempt to make my own reality more real for others, as part of an effort to transcend emotional damage. For me, words are a form of action, capable of influencing change. Their articulation represents a complete, lived experience.

But even for those people for whom language is not quite so powerful or controversial, the failure of words to convey what we need or think or feel is bound to be painful, since verbal communication is common to all of us on some level.

Talking about rage and hatred, however, can become meaningless if it loses its power to affect anything. Talking acts as a temporary stopgap, keeping some of the channels open. But when words and expressions and gestures exhaust themselves, the feelings remain in a purer and often less accessible form than ever before, and no outlet remains for rage except feeding on itself. Communication in its active sense, as part of a process of change, represents the life of a society. Communication cut off from that connection represents the death, the suicide, of that society.

If that is to be avoided, something obviously does have to change . . . first the forms of communication and then the relation of that communication to the shapes of our lives. But after that—what? Is it the society that should change? Or the nature of memory? Or the nature of experience?

The same questions always seem to intervene. And along with them there are always the doubts about whether change can ever catch up with the damage already done, the damage that has reached the saturation point in the damagee.

To me, at least, that finally became the telling point about emotional damage, mine and everyone else's. Emotional damage can almost never be expressed adequately, and the more often it is *partially* expressed, the less effect it has, until everyone grows weary of hearing the same story ("Oh no, John, women's lib was an issue *last* year") . . . until the media smooths over the gaps between pain and experience, until the most common phrase you can hear is, "I'm tired of talking about blacks and drugs and the problems of women. It's all so depressing." Quite right it's depressing . . . even more so for those who don't stop being black or women or addicts the moment the media fad fades.

Of course the person who doesn't say anything at all, but just "acts out" his or her experience, the person who looks wild-eyed and demented, the person whose rage transforms itself into violence, the person in whom venom *must* take concrete form, the person who feels there are no available outlets besides direct aggression, is not very desirable socially; in fact, is most likely to be ridiculed or ignored or "put away" or enshrined as the Fool, without anyone realizing that when words have turned to sawdust, and "constructive activity" becomes the catchall phrase for busywork, which provides the illusion of change without any of its substance, at that point there really *are* no alternatives.

I did not say any of this to the editor. Nothing about dreams or construction workers or Van Gogh or words. Nothing about emotional damage. Nothing about the "nice guys" I knew whom I couldn't bring myself to trust, no matter how good an opinion I had of them. And nothing at all about the fact that I sincerely doubted my own present or future capacity to trust any man enough to reach out for that ideal of genuine social-sexual communion which had such a claim on my imagination.

I didn't say it because I didn't know how, because it all seemed too large, too inexpressible. Besides, the editor was on his lunch hour. Certainly he seemed like a decent enough person, and that made me feel ashamed to reveal the depth of my anger, the range of my hostility. What I was even less prepared to reveal was that the Man-Hating Creature in me had put in a brief special appearance for the editor almost as soon as we started talking, an appearance provoked by the collision of longing and mistrust. Longing was an old demon, a nostalgic demon of childhood still trying to seduce a more sophisticated me. Mistrust was an adult demon, a cynic. When the two collided, hatred was inclined to intervene.

But one does not talk about child demons and adult demons over lunch in fancy restaurants. One talks about "Ideas." So I said, "Oppression does not create healthy human beings, it creates crippled ones," a remark so banal it scarcely deserved articulation. But banal or not, it was useful; it put a manageable distance between myself and the problem, disposed of some of my tension, and so abominably oversimplified the issue that I could hide behind the stereotype of my own struggle, in the meantime maintaining my safety and regaining my equilibrium. Of course, I didn't seriously think it was wholly a question of "oppression," nor wholly a question of "individual psychology" either. But rechanneling my thoughts was easier than trying to express the inexpressible.

"One doesn't cure cancer by calling it benign," I said, still teetering on the brink of the personal, still trying to steady myself on the solid soil of Ideas.

The effort collapsed instantly though, and instead of continuing I lapsed into silence while the editor waited.

Yes of course, I thought, oppression was bad. Yes of course that was why there were so few healthy blacks, whether Uncle Toms or revolutionaries, and just as few healthy women, whether satisfied suburbanites or liberationists. Yes of course, since "oppressors" were by definition not healthy either, whites and men could automatically be added to the sick list. In which case everyone was sufficiently disabled that a pall of equality might settle over us all, everyone so equally sick that they became equally healthy.

Still, not every man is an oppressor, I thought, and not every white is a racist (political rhetoric to the contrary), and the number of psychic cripples walking around—black, white, male, female—is not in direct proportion to the number of "cripplers" or even "crippling experiences," since some people seem to receive more than their share of outrages in a lifetime and yet manage to pull through it all, while other people respond with a greater degree of disturbance to a smaller number of outrages.

For the latter (myself included), more than kindness is required to uproot fear, suspicion, mistrust, and hatred. One is forced to deal with the impact of self-hatred as well, which may have become just as deeply entrenched. Since hatreds are rarely acknowledged by society as being justified, people often turn those hatreds inward (as I did in some ways), and become paralyzed by the inability to externalize their very real rage.

It is because of such complicating factors that even if every law for free abortions, community child care, and equal job opportunities were passed tomorrow and put into effect, thousands of women, perhaps millions of women (and the blacks who have been through it all already) would go on being psychologically unfit, would go on fulfilling the expectations most people* had of them, including lack of logic, superficiality, and lack of consistency or reliability . . . would continue to fulfill those roles because the roles were not quite so detachable or interchangeable as one might imagine, because they were a real part of the way people saw themselves, the way I too saw myself (why else was I always telling people how absentminded I am, making a joke of it, making it seem ten times worse than it is) . . . because, finally, those images conform to our expectations—no matter how subconscious—of what we can be, should be, and *are.* Laws and social change notwithstanding, most women would continue to use their sexuality to get them what they wanted, would continue to rely upon being sexual objects, because deep in our personal and historical past lies the belief that that's what we *are.* Learning to be something

*For women, that means men—black and white; whereas for blacks it means whites, male and female . . . which says something about the flexibility of a system in which anyone who is in one instance "oppressed" can at a moment's notice be transformed into an oppressor.

else is a long process; learning that it serves a *purpose* to be something else, that it will get you to the same place or further, is perhaps an even longer process. After all, no one expects city dwellers to arrive in the wilderness and know how to subsist on roots; no one expects them to be able to till the soil efficiently, to chuck their cultural attitudes and city ways as fast as they can put down the mortgage on their new houses. For most women, including myself, being sexy is both a tool, a weapon, and a source of pleasure. It has always guaranteed my survival in situations that were inimical to survival. And although I have often hated myself for using it, as well as hated the men who were so easily moved by it and by almost nothing else, I have still learned to rely upon it. So could I easily surrender that mechanism of survival which enabled me to grow into a fairly strong weed in the middle of concrete? Yes I could, but with difficulty, and *only* if I thought more human behavior could achieve the same results. Undoubtedly, being able to do *that* would also make me able to surrender a good deal of mistrust, hostility, and desire for power, since sex, or rather the alluring package of sex, is one of the few things that give women real power over men. It is, in addition, I think, one of the prime sources of female ambivalence: astonishment that men can be so easily seduced and contempt for the fact that it requires such a second-rate skill, which in its "natural" state would not be a skill at all, but an expression of deep feelings.

As long as sex remains such an important commodity for women, no matter what reforms are enacted, most women, I think, will continue, with varying degrees of frequency and intensity, to feel hatred and contempt for men, since their minds can be controlled through their penises, instead of the other way around (which might be a corollary to the old adage that the way to a man's heart is through his stomach). Most women will continue to *use* that distorted mix to get us what we want, even as we are appalled by the reduction of experience it represents.

Freud said that you don't give up one pleasure unless you have another to replace it. True, you don't give up the distorted pleasures of packaged sex unless you can be satisfied by something more genuine. You don't break up your marriage because you decide that being married is by definition "unliberated" or because you think marriage is an "obsolete institution" (those women who claim to be doing so are fooling themselves, and acting out of needs far deeper, far more personal, and far more complex). You don't stop acting like a sex object because you conclude that it is ultimately degrading, nor do you stop sometimes wishing you were a man because you now think that being a woman is just as good if not better. And you don't stop hating men because hate is destructive to yourself and others.

If women are to change, then we have to see that something in the attitude of men also changes. (A man I know, on reaching his fortieth birthday, said that it was great to arrive at an age when he would no longer be at the mercy of his penis. One hopes it wouldn't take quite so long for everyone.) For if things don't change, if biology cannot be harnessed to serve the needs of human beings, then we risk an anger so large as to be ultimately paralyzing, risk the solidification of a gap that closes us off completely from what every human being needs most: love.

The scars in our psyches will not heal overnight though. By and large we will continue to carry them with us, the scars of habits deeply ingrained, of experiences never wholly assimilated, of a character which has been forming since the day we were born. Ultimately, it is precisely our willingness to experiment with our own lives that has made us a marked generation.

"There are always scars, you know," I say to the editor, having been silent for a long time.

"Scars?" he says.

"Yes, scars. Things that don't get better, or at least don't go away. Even when they're 'cured.' It's not that I think everything is going to stay the same. It's just that the expectations . . . well, they're limited, all things considered."

"Oh," he says. "I think I see what you mean. You mean that even though you're relatively healthy, you still have problems."

"Sort of," I say. And think: Well, so much for emotional damage.

The editor looks at me with a mixture of sympathy and understanding. "I understand," he says. "I really do."

I nod and smile. Whereupon a perfect ringer of unadvertised and unsolicited hatred settles like an iron halo about my head.

. . .

This hatred which appears fast on the heels of "understanding" is a peculiar thing, though extremely common, I suspect. I have felt it, a positive storm of it, when sitting in a room listening to a man talk about his sympathy for the women's movement . . . about how he understood what a terribly destructive thing this "oppression" was . . . about how awful it must be to have men poking at you on the streets, in subways, on the beach . . . about how he knew men had a lot to learn . . . about how we were all going to struggle to change the world so men and women could live happily ever after.

I have felt it, too, while sitting in the living room of a painter couple I know. The woman was groping her way through her hostility toward men artists who refused to take her seriously, saying that she didn't care whether or not they thought her work was really good, that she just wanted them to respect the seriousness of her intent, something they would grant automatically to one another. But as the conversation progressed, the problem came closer to home. There were two studios in their apartment, one large, one small. Her husband had the larger one.

"Well *someone* has to have the small one," she said. "And why shouldn't it be me? But then why *should* it be me?"

"Yes, why should it?" I asked.

"Well he's older," she said. "He's been established a lot longer than I have . . . I suppose . . ." her voice trailed off for a moment.

"But it's not only that," she said. "Even if I had the

studio, I wouldn't use it as much as I should. There's shopping, the children, so many things . . ."

At that point her husband walked in. He sat down while his wife continued discussing the issue. But her tone had changed. Whereas before she had been guarded against the force of her own emotions and was trying to be rational, now she was guarded against the effect those emotions might have on her husband. Instead of one struggle, she now had two. And her husband, watching her build to the point where she said, "And you know about the studios?" was wonderfully understanding—admirable in fact.

"Of course, you're right," he said. "It's always bothered me. Would you like to take the other studio?"

"But where would you work?" she said, floundering in her sense of being "unfair" to him.

"I could take another studio," he said, "on the outside."

There was a long pause, and then she said, "Would you be willing to teach the extra hours in order to pay for it?"

"Teach extra hours?" he said. "Well why should I? I already teach more hours than I want to."

And that was when "It" first came into focus. He had conceded everything she asked, which made her feel guilty for being foolish and demanding, for asking. But still there was some unfocused grievance, some unfocused source of hostility which had lost its justification when he agreed with her. Somehow the whole thing had a quality of "sacrifice" for her, even though for *him* it was a real attempt to see through his own conditioning. But at the moment when he was being the most understanding, the expression of hostility in her eyes had been the most powerful, and she had topped her perfectly reasonable argument with one which was perfectly unreasonable, instead of pointing out, for example, that he might use the smaller studio, as she had been doing. At that point, though, she had needed to stretch herself beyond being "realistic" in order to take care of a slow swell of generalized anger which had begun to shift inside of her like a glacier, anger that was now directed toward him precisely because he "understood" and was trying to be charitable. On the surface, at least, there was no longer a *good reason* to be angry. Except for the fact that people who are dependent on someone else's kindness for the satisfaction of their own needs, invariably feel irrational surges of hostility toward their benefactors. The relations between men and women are such that no matter how much a man does, his efforts are almost always tinged with this quality of being self-righteously generous, instead of the quality of just doing what is natural. If he was generous then she was supposed to be grateful. But who wants to be grateful to one's husband for doing what he should have been doing all along? Yet even those women who *are* grateful, examine their own reactions and think, "My God, what a pitiable thing this gratefulness is, what a settling for crumbs," and feel an immediate surge of just the opposite emotion: fury.

The wife undoubtedly felt that even if she had lost *one* reason for being angry, there must be a hundred, a thousand *other* good reasons. But it was worthless to be hostile for reasons that existed only in the abstract. Given the current state of things, a man was guilty no matter *what* he did. If you were married, though, and loved your husband and were angry, you usually told him why you were angry and then proceeded to thrash it out. If you had no reason to be angry, then you restrained yourself and tried to stop being angry.

Except she hadn't stopped being angry. In fact, if anything, she was even angrier than before, when with a large part of her (the part that had felt generous and guilty), she had taken his side, thereby justifying the part of her that felt hostile . . . since out of the generosity and the hostility came some sort of balance.

But if *he* were understanding, and not only understanding but helpful to boot, then he took away not only her anger, but also the "generosity" which had justified it . . . and, on top of that, gave her the added burden of *his* generosity—so that now he looked good whereas she looked bad.

Certainly that kind of mess was common enough. And it was all tangled up with this ambivalence over being understood. (I by the way had felt a sympathetic surge of hostility toward him when she felt hostile, and then a surge of hostility toward her for making herself seem foolish. The simple categorizer in me would have liked at that point to see the thing settled on a more liberated-woman-gains-victory-in-the-home basis, whereas now the issue was considerably muddied—that is, humanized by the fact that two complicated and contradictory personalities were involved.) Still, despite my *own* contradictory responses, I really did understand how she felt for a very plain reason: I too am a woman. And have been through that kind of hostility. Often.

But why, I asked myself, why should we (I) react so negatively when we get exactly what we think we want? Why is there always this residue of rage left over? Is it because we cherish with some part of ourselves this pet cancer (which in her case may not be a cancer at all)? Is it because being neurotic you know how to protect your neurosis from anyone who attempts to interfere with it? Is it because I/we don't really want to be understood? Or is it because understanding is so full of contradictions in itself that the resopnses to it are inevitably contradictory as well?

The answer, I thought, was probably yes to all of these questions.

But there was also another answer. A great many women felt hostility toward men who "understood" simply because no matter how much they understood they still remained men. And that meant that as soon as they were removed from the particular situation in which they were being understanding, they had a protective coloration which women didn't have. In other words, the husband, whether he had the larger studio or the smaller, would not walk out the door to meet other artists who didn't take him seriously even though he had been painting for many years. Instead, his friends often commented on how much he had influenced his wife, even though by his own admission, they had influenced each other . . . commented on the quality of "his" show, which was really hers and had a few supplementary drawings of his in it. His work and its value would be *assumed.* And in her case, she could only win a "symbolic victory" of gaining the larger studio, but would still have to walk out the door and not be taken seriously by *anyone.*

As for the editor, once he walked out of the restaurant, he, too, was still a man. He would not have to pass construction workers who would remark on the size of his cock. On the other hand, when I walked out the door, it could be *predicted* that within five minutes *someone* would be sure to remark on my "tits," or else a well-groomed man, who might look very much like the editor, would start walking alongside of me gaping at my body. It could be *predicted* that if the two of us were to walk down the street together and were to stop a random stranger to ask, "What do you think our relationship is?" that they would assume I was either his wife, his girlfriend, his secretary, or any combination of those. No one would be surprised to learn that he was an editor, though they might very well be surprised to learn I was a writer. (Many men, when told that I'm a writer, respond by asking whether I work for a woman's magazine—the *Ladies' Home Journal* perhaps?) Which is probably the reason why I feel strangely split after having conferences with editors during which my ego thrives and then walking out on the street to become once again "the body." As a result, I am somewhat inclined to wave metaphorical banners of my seriousness in the face of anyone who does not immediately acknowledge it.

Once, when I was living with a painter on a Greek

island, we had an argument about my assertiveness. Every time we met people they would ask him what he did. They never asked me the same question. It was assumed that I was with him . . . which was quite enough for me to be doing. As a result, I got into the disagreeable habit of interrupting to say that *I* was a writer. Many people (the polite ones) would simply raise their eyebrows or not comment on my obvious need to account for myself. The painter, on the other hand, since he lived with me, didn't think it was necessary to be polite. He told me that I should stop doing things like that, since they made me look bad. He insisted that if I didn't keep on telling people what I did, they would eventually ask me. I insisted that they wouldn't. So we tried it out, and of course, no one ever bothered to ask. Which surprised him. But he still found it disagreeable for me to assert myself, so that whenever people asked him what he did, he would answer that he was a painter and would add that I was a writer. The result was that people usually gave me a cursory nod, as if to acknowledge my existence, and then went on to ask him more about his work.

Certainly he understood more than he had before. But the nature of my own bind was unchanged by his understanding, since there was no way of implementing the understanding without being conspicuous or combative, both of which made him uncomfortable.

Unfortunately, I have found that the only time my separate identity is assured is when I am living alone, working and earning my own living. People are so often surprised to learn that I am completely dependent upon my own resources, that they prod me in search of evidence that would prove at least *some* link between me and an invisible male who is helping me out. If they respond that way even when there is no evidence for their assumptions, imagine how easily those assumptions can be made within a more traditional structure. Inevitably, then, when I am living with a man, my identity shrinks to a quarter of its normal size, and I become, even if not explicitly, an appendage.

The truth of the matter is that the editor's and the husband's and the painter's and all men's understanding of the "female condition" is separated from the condition itself, separated from the daily monotonous and repetitious occurrences which reinforce that condition. And as soon as they stop talking to the woman they "understand," they are able to go about their business thinking about something *other* than the condition of women, whereas the moment I attempt to go about *my* business, I am obstructed in some way and am forced to deal with that condition simply because I am a woman and will be a woman long after publishing houses stop putting out books about us.

So I react with outrage to "understanding" males, even though I think that genuine insight is more to be desired than just about anything, even though I appreciate the efforts involved and appreciate the sincerity of those efforts.

No man can fully understand what it means to be a woman, just as no woman can fully understand what it means to be a man. (That mysterious lack of understanding, which is comprised of fascination, bewilderment, anger, and alienation, may well be at the heart of what we call an attraction to the opposite sex, although it is *also* at the heart of man-hating and, I suppose, woman-hating.)

In addition to all that, though, there is the simple fact that I personally react badly to all assumptions about understanding, since most people seem to think that it is something to be acquired quickly, easily, and with a minimum of effort. Reading a single newspaper's ongoing reports on Vietnam is enough to make most people think they understand the war. Having a black friend is enough to make most people think they understand blacks. Attending a university is enough to make one understand how it functions. Working in a mental institution or having a mental patient in the family is equal to understanding mental illness. Knowing someone who has been in analysis or being in it oneself or reading a couple of books by Freud or Jung means understanding psychology.

But anyone, I should think, who would be the recipient of such facile understanding, anyone who was told that their situation was understood would be bound to resent the assumptions that underlie the assertion, since understanding is one of the most complicated aims that human beings can struggle to achieve. (Not even considering the equally common fact that adolescents hate their parents whether their parents understand them or not, and often hate them even more if they understand too much, while employees hate employers no matter how understanding they are, mental patients hate psychiatrists and blacks hate liberals more than rednecks precisely *because* they presume to understand more.)

Understanding, like hatred, is not something you can bounce up against a wall like a rubber ball. Nor is it something you can acquire in a crash course and discuss over coffee or cocktails. As with reading Dostoevsky, the Monarch College Notes just won't do.

For understanding is a process, and all processes take time and experience to give them a shape.

It is not mere chance, I think, that the process of going through analysis requires so much repetition of the same things before one gets to understand much of anything. Nor is it mere chance that at some point, when one is talking most dispassionately and articulately about things that hurt, one recognizes a refusal to *let* those things hurt, to get in touch with them . . . and then one has to go through the whole process all over again, until finally, when the hurt has come into contact with its source, the words come out like smashed slivers of crystal.

Most of the common varieties of "understanding" are cheap. Translating what aches inside of you so fiercely that you sometimes want to faint is never cheap. It's always expensive.

So invariably, when someone tries to inject me with a dosage of understanding, I wind up being allergic to them, along with what they have to say, and in addition, end up being unbearably conscious of the precise cookie-cutter shapes communication takes in this world of ours, so freshly dedicated to tolerance in the name of social progress.

The problem of being understood rapidly amplifies when one realizes there are certain characteristics that are usually thought of as being innately female . . . particularly: softness and passivity and tolerance. Clearly, it is far more "pleasant" and more "understandable" when women keep "in character," when we speak of suffering in dulcet feminine voices . . . or when we don't speak of it at all (since no one these days wants to sound like the long-suffering Jewish mother) . . . or when we emphasize that we *do not* hate men, but in fact really *love* them.

And, of course, most women would rather please men than displease them. But therein lies the real snag. Women who *must* express their anger, their hostility, their hatred . . . women who are used to being accommodating, who have some affection for those qualities that are best in themselves, who are used to talking about their anger as if it were something they had picked up by accident along the roadside, those women—and I am one—are particularly susceptible to the notion of being "understood," since being understood helps to prevent conflict (which is unpleasant) and helps to smooth over the rough edges. And for a man there is nothing easier than listening to a woman talk about her anger, when that anger is directed toward generalized principles . . . just so long as it is *not* directed toward *him* personally, toward the man across the table at dinner, the man in bed with her, the man with whom she shares two and a half children. But if we are going to be honest, there are, I think, relatively few women whose real hatred is directed toward the question of whether or not the right laws have been passed on their behalf, since legality is no more than a concept, just as discrimination is a concept. And real anger is not directed at concepts but at people, at the people who make those concepts vivid and painful in one's own life. In this case, those people are more often than not male, more often than not the males one knows best, the males with whom the repetition of seemingly trivial conflicts can become the substance of a growing awareness that *something* is wrong . . . the men with whom man-hating is a real and unavoidable issue.

When I was a child, I used to have knockdown, drag-out fights with my younger brother, in which we usually wound up under the grand piano trying to crush each other's bones to smithereens. After ten or fifteen minutes of such warfare, it became obvious that even though he was younger, he was also more wiry, and eventually managed to get me flat on my back with him sitting on my chest. Exhausted from the struggle I would lie there and whisper, "Peace," not meaning it for a second, since if anything, I harbored even greater hostility toward him than before. In that position, however, peace was the only offer I could make. My parents of course were pleased when such treaties were put into effect. My brother was pleased because peace to him meant victory. Only I was miserable. Peace to me meant only one thing—surrender.

Among men and women, such illusions of "peace" and "understanding" can all too easily be used as defensive weapons to avoid conflict, since in life people usually prefer to take whatever shortcuts they can find to happiness.

For myself, though, I think that at this point I would prefer less understanding and less peace, would prefer men to stop claiming to understand more than they do, would prefer them to stop trying to grease the wheels of progress with packaged comprehension, even if the creaks and grinds that result are intolerable to both our ears, even if the true progress that results is only one-tenth of what the illusory progress was.

And if that means that a man I like is going to confess to being scared and confused about women, or to not understanding a goddamn thing about us although he would like very much to understand . . . maybe then we can start to talk.

We had almost finished eating lunch when the editor said, "It's nice to be around a woman who knows where she stands but is still cooperative. I must admit that I have difficulty with some of the other women, the man-hating types."

"Yes," I said. "It's very hard for you to be the object of a hostility you don't think you deserve. But on the other hand—"

"Of course," the editor interrupted, smiling warmly, "there is a lot to be done. I can see it in myself . . . I'm not much of a male chauvinist, but still there are reflexes . . ."

The smile escaped me again. Yes, I thought. That's true. There *are* reflexes. And I am a hypocrite, or at the very least a coward.

4

There is another kind of understanding that is often offered in exchange for deep change. It is not the understanding of individual men, but the understanding of official institutions, an understanding to which it is difficult if not impossible to respond. An example of what this new climate of understanding has produced is the passage of liberalized abortion laws. Now, how can one object to such a "humanization" of the lives of women? One can't, of course, except for the fact that nothing is humane when it is not in the hands of human beings. Abortions do not change the substantial basis of the relationship between the sexes—the *felt* basis of that relationship—and like the birth control pill, they are capable of insuring *only* that one will not have to endure heavy physical consequences as a result of those relationships.

I wonder whether the fact that a woman can get an abortion now with relative ease will change another fact, which is that pregnancy is a state of mind as much as a physical condition. Will it change the fact that the experience of being abandoned by a man is what frequently produces the need for an abortion in the first place? And that such desertions in themselves are closely connected to feelings of man-hating? Will it change the fact that the more "efficient" an abortion is, the more it makes the feelings connected with abortions seem irrelevant? Will it change the fact that for many women, the adaptation to the physical fact of being aborted, requires another adaptation . . . a sense of separation from the life of her body? Abortions may give women greater control over their own bodies, but they also, and perhaps more importantly, give women less of a sense of relationship to their bodies, and less of a possibility for dealing with any of the feelings (fear, anger, need, hatred) that accompany the mere *idea* of having an abortion.

I am reminded of an experience I had several months ago with a young girl from the Midwest who had come to New York for her abortion. She was a freshman in college, and had a sweet, snub-nosed face. Her abortion was scheduled for noon somewhere out in the suburbs. A friend of mine asked me whether I could drive her out to the appointment. I could.

Sitting in the car, she said, "My parents charged the guy with rape. Brought the whole thing into court. In my state all you have to do is be in the same house with a man for over ten minutes if you're underage and they can get him. So we stood up in court and promised to be good for three months. That got him off. But I was being watched all the time. Couldn't go and smoke a joint without being sure I'd get busted. Couldn't fuck or do anything. So as soon as the three months were up, we got back together . . . and now . . . well, here I am."

I looked at her sideways, wondering at the toughness in her, at the fierce casualness, at the deliberate absence of feeling.

"How many months . . . I mean weeks . . . pregnant are you?" I asked.

"Oh about ten," she said. "That's still the early stage. Early enough that I don't have to go to the hospital." Her face was extremely calm, seemingly innocent of all knowledge. "They take it out with one of those vacuum things," she said. "The doctor told me I wouldn't feel any pain at all. Just afterward, a little bit, but it would be like cramps, that's all."

A vacuum thing, I thought. The very thought made me a little bit nauseated. Suck. And instantly the "thing" was gone . . . the moment when his semen squirted into her and collided with the egg totally obliterated. I wondered what it had been like for them that day or that night. Whether the sex had been fierce or tender or passionate or indifferent. Whether they had gotten up and put their clothes on and walked out of the house, whether he had spent the night with her, whether they had done it between classes, whether they loved or liked each other. Wondered, in short, what the connection between the sexual act and the sexual consequence was.

My mind reverted to the image of the vacuum.

"Somehow just thinking about it makes me a little bit sick," I said. "I keep getting a visual picture."

"Yes, I know," she said very softly.

I was suddenly appalled at my own lack of tact or understanding. I had expressed my thoughts without taking into consideration any of the conflicts she must be feeling. Maybe I had done it with the hidden intent of bringing out those conflicts, which she would certainly be better off without, at least at this particular moment. Somewhere inside of me I had been more concerned with finding out about her sense of connection than I was with making her feel comfortable. And that was unfair to her. But unfair or not, it still tapped something real, something that had no place in our expedition. And that something was feeling. She had been "reassured" by a doctor . . . the operation would not be painful . . . it was just a "little thing." And this scientific assurance was supposed to dispose of fear and anxiety. On the surface of course it did. On the surface, Janet was composed, was thoroughly prepared for her abortion. She was a model patient. She was a symbol of the triumph of modern medical technology and modern legal enlightenment.

But somewhere inside of her, she was also a scared kid. Somewhere inside of her she *must* feel the absence of the boy who had made her pregnant, if she cared for him, and if she didn't care for him, then she must feel the absence of that caring, or must hate him for having been responsible for this business which taxed so severely her ability to deal rationally with her own life. Somewhere inside of her, she must think it strange that tomorrow she would be going back to her summer job, that tomorrow the whole thing would be over with, done, completed, forgotten. And if she didn't feel any of those things, then she was really in trouble, because it meant, it had to mean, that she had repressed every bit of psychic consequence that having an abortion implied, had repressed all personal emotion from the experience, had coated herself so thoroughly with a veneer of sophistication that none of this was going to get through.

But of course, she hadn't done that. Her soft "I know" was sufficient testimony to that.

"Janet, I'm sorry," I said. "I'm not being much help. That was a terrible thing to say."

"That's OK," she said, keeping her eyes straight in front of her. "I try not to think about any of it."

I was on the verge of tears. What could I really provide for her at that moment? Could I say, as the doctors had said, "Everything's going to be all right. Just relax and don't worry"? Could I offer sympathy and thus upset that delicate balance of strength and detachment that she was so dependent upon? Could I talk about something else and pretend that none of this was really going to happen? Could I ask her about the boy?

I couldn't do any of those things. The fact that I was taking her to have an abortion precluded the possibilities of my doing anything else. It forced me to deny to myself that my casual "Of course," when my friend asked me to take Janet to the doctor, had been a lie. It forced me to deny that even if Janet was able to cope with this thing, *I wasn't.* It forced me to acknowledge that a helpful detachment was the only thing that could be of any use to Janet right now, and that I didn't possess that helpful detachment.

I'm being old fashioned, I thought. I'm being sentimental. I'm investing the whole business with an emotional weight that it just doesn't have any more. I'm letting the cheap paperback abortion stories get to me. But, as usual, paperback stories, no matter how melodramatic they are, carry along with them germs of truth, vestiges of feelings so powerful that they shrink from facile articulation.

Janet is eighteen years old, I thought. What could she possibly do with a child? Of course she shouldn't have a baby. Of course abortions make sense. But even if they do make sense, something is wrong with a world in which girls have abortions, rushed through nicely and efficiently. Motherhood cannot be taken all that lightly. Not even in the name of equality and efficiency. Which was not to say that I thought the abortion law should be repealed, or that I thought Janet was wrong to get an abortion, or that eighteen-year-old girls should be abstinent.

It was only to say that abortions existed within a context, and that context was only secondarily legal and medical. Its primary context remained, as it always had, in the realm of the human and the personal. Its primary context had to do with the quality of the relationships between men and women.

And that primary context was what was being consciously and deliberately *ignored.*

I didn't mention any of that to Janet. My single comment had been bad enough already.

What I did instead was try to find out indirectly what her situation was. I asked her about the boy.

"I dug him," she said. "We went through a lot of shit

together. But when all this came down with my parents, he got fed up. He stuck with me for a while. I figured we might get married. But after I was pregnant, he decided to split. I can't say that I blame him."

That was fairly typical, I thought. Thousands of girls her age and younger were going through the same thing: a close physical and emotional relationship with a boy, parents who fought against those relationships, rebellions from the kids, pregnancies, split-ups . . . and a future of new relationships, new pregnancies, new split-ups, new relationships.

"How come you didn't take pills or anything?" I asked.

There was a very long pause before she answered. "I don't know," she said. "I guess maybe in a way I wanted a kid. I mean I wanted *his* kid. But . . ." She didn't finish the sentence. "Anyway," she said, "I wasn't ready to have a kid. So an abortion's the best thing now. And we probably wouldn't have made it together. I mean we weren't ready to really settle down. It was sort of like playing house in a way. I thought having a baby would take care of a lot of things."

I didn't say anything. Hadn't I, after all, thought the same thing when I had been her age and in love? "A baby," I'd thought. "All that love. We'd be a family." Of course, I'd been willing to ignore the fact that the man already had a family of his own. And that having a baby at that point was a substitute for being a baby myself . . . that wanting someone to take care of and love was a substitute for wanting someone to take care of and love me. All of those things I'd been unable to see then. And having the baby of someone I loved, whether I was ready for it or not, seemed like a very romantic thing to do.

Luckily I never became pregnant. And didn't have to decide whether or not to have the baby. But the need out of which the desire for a child had grown did not evaporate. And would not have evaporated if I had become pregnant and been able to have an abortion. The need, fundamentally, was for love. My perceptions of what signified love were somewhat distorted, but they were, to me at least, real.

Probably Janet had similar perceptions. They were put in a more sophisticated framework, sex being somewhat more taken for granted than it had been when I was her age. But fundamentally they remained unchanged, whether the two of them had "gone through a lot of shit together" or not.

Chances were that whether she admitted it or not, whether she could say casually, "I really don't blame him," or not, she still felt at least *some* hostility toward her boyfriend for having ditched her. Chances were that she felt *a lot* of hostility, which had been smothered under a sexual tolerance and "respect for other people's freedom," which was so much the current coin of the realm.

After all, if her boyfriend wanted to split, that was his right. She was never going to push him to do something he didn't want to do. She was never going to demand anything. She was going to be independent enough to handle her own life. And lonely enough to get pregnant again in six months. Or maybe not. One never could be sure.

Still, I had been pseudo-sophisticated enough at the ages of fifteen through eighteen to know something about what was concealed underneath the pose of total independence. And although I had to assume that some people were more stable than I was at that age, I couldn't make that assumption about Janet. There was too much that was familiar in what she said.

We used a different language to describe our experiences. But outside of that, the differences were really not considerable. I probably would have said to the father, "You have no responsibility for me. I'll have the baby and bring it up myself," meanwhile hoping desperately that he would offer to stick with me. And she would probably have said, "Split, man. It's a groove. I can take care of myself." Maybe she would have meant it. And maybe she meant it when she expressed the opinion that an abortion was nothing . . . an attitude that in itself would seem to be a consequence of the fairly widespread belief that sex too is nothing. Of course, if it is really nothing, then we have lost a channel of expression which has been capable of bringing out the very worst and sometimes the very best in us. Of course, too, something that is nothing can never be a source of man-hating.

When we got to the doctor's office, I asked Janet whether she wanted me to pick her up later in the afternoon. She said no; she was flying back to the Midwest and would get a cab to the airport. She was sure everything would be fine.

I talked to my friend later in the day. She said that Janet had waited all afternoon and had been told that she would probably be the last one taken, since there was quite a long line of women ahead of her. There was a possibility that she would have to come back the following day. The following day, my friend hadn't heard anything more from her, but she assumed that, as Janet had predicted, everything was fine.

I guess it probably was.

In my neighborhood, deep in the slums, it is generally acknowledged among the kids that sex is fun and doesn't cost as much as dope. That certainly is, or can be, true. Except, according to one boy I know who "scores every chick in sight," things aren't always quite that simple.

Most of the girls he "screws" don't use contraceptives. They want to get away from home, and being pregnant is a good method. Usually, though, they panic when the dream becomes a reality, when they discover that the father ("That's me," my friend says proudly) has no intention of marrying them or even accepting paternity. "I'm fifteen," he says. "I just wanna fuck. So I says to them, 'Who me? C'mon baby. You ballin' fifty guys on the street.' That always takes care of it. Besides, they just gotta go an' get an abortion. It's nothin'."

For him, the crash availability of abortions has been a real bonus. But for an enormous number of girls who thought of themselves as free, it has been just the beginning of a discovery that they are, in reality, quite hopelessly bound.

The tendency to postpone things until the last minute is common to most of us, and since planning sex is inimical to the modern image of spontaneity, many girls get abortions because they didn't plan to have sex in the first place. Or else they get abortions because, on principle, they wouldn't buy contraceptives, since they intend to be "pure" anyway. But when the chips are down and the boyfriend says, "If you won't, baby, there's a thousand chicks out there who will," her principles slide rapidly out of focus. Which means that she starts out helpless and ends up helpless.

How many women, I wonder, get abortions because they're in situations that give men power and make women powerless? How many are the consequences of rapes, seductions, "boyfriends in love," or cruisers? How many are a result of situations that breed man-hating? How many women fall in love, are rejected, and out of a desperate desire to resurrect feelings that no longer exist, become pregnant in order to fulfill that desire? For how many women are abortions a reflection of the fact that they know they've been in some way used by men? How many women, in short, have abortions because an illusion of love existed in their imaginations, an illusion that turned out to be pure fraud?

It is undoubtedly true that a great many women become pregnant without ever having loved *anyone,* not even themselves . . . become pregnant because in some as yet uncrystallized corners of their minds, they believe that having a child is the way out of an empty life—while other women became pregnant as an expression of indifference, or an expression of rage toward their own bodies or rage toward men.

But no matter what pregnancy is an expression of, it is always an expression of a need more complicated than the needs that abortions can satisfy. It is always an expression of the hidden stubbornness of humanity in the face of machinery, humanity at its best and at its worst. And whether a "vacuum thing" is used or not, there is a *mental* image of being pregnant that bypasses entirely the stage when "the baby isn't *really* a baby."

For myself I know that on the occasions when I've thought that maybe I was pregnant, the first image that flashed into my mind was of the baby already born. Being pregnant, in my own mind, equals life. And the second I become pregnant, that life exists for me, whether that is scientifically verifiable or not. That's not to say that the life shouldn't be aborted. But it is to insist that psychologically it could never be "the expulsion of a dot." And psychologically I could never be free of the memory of *someone* who was inside of me at the right or wrong moment.

"Enlightened" societies such as ours, however, are fond of capsulizing problems. In New York, a woman gets pregnant . . . she decides not to have the baby . . . she has an abortion and goes home twenty-four hours later, having avoided the concrete anguish of looking for an abortionist, paying exorbitant fees, public shame, having a baby against her will, and fear of being butchered. Presto! A problem is solved.

Nothing about the anguish she still must feel when she

goes home and looks in the mirror and thinks, "It's gone" (despite her knowledge that it was not "really" a human life inside of her). Nothing about the anguish because the man didn't bother to stick around, or the sense of alienation from herself involved in the thought that she doesn't really know or care who the father was. Nothing about the protective and modern "indifference" she may have felt for the whole procedure. Nothing about the sense of unreality that pervades the idea of going back to work. Nothing about the fact that all of the questions she never resolved in relation to herself as a woman are *still* unresolved. Nothing about the fact that a general callousness in human relationships is what makes abortions necessary in the first place.

I remember a conversation I had with a friend the day the New York abortion law was passed. She was working as a secretary in a publishing house and when I stopped by for lunch, she was reading the newspaper. I looked over her shoulder to see what she was reading. It was the article on the abortion law. "What do you think?" I said naively, carried away with a sense of "progress." "Isn't it wonderful?"

She looked up and I could see in her face the struggle between opposing tendencies. On the one hand, the desire to seem casual, and on the other hand, her own personal bitterness, too profound to be repressed. The bitterness won out. She spoke slowly with a kind of venom in her voice. "I had mine last year. But I have plenty of friends who will have them this year. All I want to know is, what are they going to do about our memories, our fucked-up memories and our fucked-up minds? Are they going to pay us psychological indemnities for breakdowns, panics, disgust, and fear? They ought to have an article on *that.*" She laughed shortly. "Abortion law, huh. Big deal."

I remembered how cynical she always was, how unapproachable to strangers, how she mistrusted everyone she came in contact with. I remembered how pleased I had been a few hours before when I learned of the "legal landmark." And knew that my response was finally shallow, for closer to home, as usual, legalities mean very little, and for her, more than an aboriton per se had been at stake. The quality of her life had been at stake ultimately, and about one's own life, one can rarely afford to be fair-minded and disinterested.

Which brought back another memory. It was of a girl I'd known at college who became pregnant. She had been involved with two men simultaneously, one of them a brilliant, much respected scientist. She was not at all sure whom the child belonged to, and her uncertainty provided both males with the ideal out . . . they both disclaimed responsibility. Her family, respectable, middle class, arranged for an abortion. A few days later, she slashed her wrists with a slab of glass, and a week later, I found her, her wrists still bound, wandering through the hallway, a dazed expression on her face, the piece of glass in her hand again. I coaxed her into turning the glass over to me, trying as hard as I could to be gentle. "Your life is still worth something, you know," I said. She didn't answer for a moment. Then finally she said, "Yeah," as if she were considering the worth of a can of cold vichyssoise.

Later in the evening she cried. "The bastards," she sobbed. "I hate them. I hate both of them. And men are all alike."

Physically her abortion had certainly been comfortable, routine even. But something had remained, and would remain, would still be there when I saw her again several years later. That something could not be vacuumed out. It was hatred. And it was lodged deep in her brain, like a bullet.

5

There are times when I wonder whether nature isn't really the one to hold responsible. It seems a lot easier to blame nature than to blame men (although blaming society runs a close second), and often I find myself thinking that perhaps the rigors of biology will at least succeed in reducing the pain of the personal. I conclude that the real trouble derives from the fact that men and women are vitally different, not in those ways which provide for an interesting variety, but in ways which make of sexuality a veritable war zone. At moments when I despair, when man-hating fills up the space between me and my opposite number, I conclude that we are up against the barrier reef of an anatomical destiny which yields nothing to sensibility.

Among men, the sex drive often leads an autonomous life, completely separate from the drive for love. Among women the two drives are usually much more closely related. Since love is scarce as hen's teeth, most men will settle for pleasure, while many women will either persist in abstinence or else feel some form of inner split after having sex which satisfies just physical needs. (The woman who claims to be doing it because she likes to and *no more,* and who ends up more deeply entangled than she ever expected to be, is a perfect example of this, as is the woman who finds she has a growing attachment to a man with whom she has sex, while the man has a decreasing one.

In that area, one of the real differences between us seems to have something to do with a woman's relationship to growth and gestation, a relationship which is usually of secondary importance to a man. For women the *need* for growth and gestation seems to be extremely powerful and perhaps even innate. It is undoubtedly connected to the whole process of reproduction, and exists whether potential babies are involved or not . . . may exist even more strongly when they are not.

Gestation, of course, is a complex inner process in which sexuality is fed by everything else a woman has at her disposal, much in the same way that she might feed a fetus. When there is no fetus, an inclusive kind of sexual intimacy fills up a comparable inner space. But when sex is separated from that context, the disparity between a penetration that is no more than an "action" and a penetration that reaches into complex inner space can become quite overwhelming. And certainly has been for me.

To most men the problem undoubtedly does not seem very real. To them the clearest aim of sex is orgasm, that moment of intense physical intimacy and satisfaction which so often serves as a substitute for other kinds of intimacy. Perhaps that is one of the reasons why men seem to be so concerned with satisfying women sexually and interpret that satisfaction in terms of what they think would satisfy them if they were women. It may also be one of the reasons why men seem to think that many women can never be completely satisfied sexually. The terrain where a woman remains forever unsatisfied or even, as they say, "insatiable," is probably the area where her sexuality borders most closely on that more complex psychosexual area of her being. An area that of course can't be satisfied by a simple act, no matter how sophisticated or prolonged it may be.

Thinking about such differences in needs and orientation can be a very painful thing. The mind protests. I find myself thinking, well, it can't be that Nature designed us to have mutually irreconcilable needs, designed us for the kinds of conflicts that would ultimately destroy all of our capacities for shared experience, designed us not for the mystery of difference, but the agony of difference.

It seems to me, though, that I am always coming up against variations of the same things, no matter what kinds of minds or what kinds of characters are involved. With men who are more sensitive and men who are less sensitive the problem still emerges. It is all well and good to say, Down with the double standard, women can screw as much as they want to, can have as many love affairs as men. But what happens when a woman doesn't *want* to have love affairs, as many women don't, and their husbands or boyfriends say, "But you have a perfect right to if I'm going to." What should she do? Have an affair just to prove that she's equal to him? Tell him that he can't have affairs? Or just smother her feelings and accept things as they are?

Accede to nature or fight against it?

And what of those few men whose impulses have "naturally" developed in such a way that they really are in some important sense dissatisfied sexually with a relationship that falls short of expressing strong feeling . . . not necessarily love, but at least some sort of *personal* commitment? Usually they too suffer from the myths that surround the idea of male potency, and because our definitions of what is natural seem more like aberrations than variations, men often think of themselves as sexually inadequate.

For me at least, a sexuality that is *somewhat* restrained has become a cornerstone of sexual consideration (not a consideration that is the result of damaging repression or "duty" but out of some kind of deeper, corresponding, *mutual* realization grounded in mutual respect). I have usually found that those men who could be relied on to possess a high degree of sexual empathy had major problems of their own . . . either they were afraid of women, had difficulty giving up their virginity, were worried about "not being able to get it up," felt guilty about sex in the first place, couldn't stand being intimate with a woman they also liked, or else were just shy and awkward.

With men like that I could relax and feel safe. Except in the long run I had to confess that I didn't want to feel safe. I just wanted to feel human. I didn't want to limit my life to relations with men whose "understanding" of women was defined by their fear of women or their inability to respond to women. I didn't want to think that my own psychic well-being was dependent upon the psychic incapacities of others, upon *their* pain or ambivalence.

What I wanted was to become healthy again myself. What I wanted was someone to be healthy *with* (if ever I got back to that point). What I wanted was to discover men who were passionate but also understood restraint; men who were sexually competent but capable of choosing whom to be competent with; men who realized from something within themselves (not something imposed on them) that mind, body, and spirit need to be integrated before body can involve itself deeply; men who could say yes and no; men for whom such a choice really exists.

To me, that is what a man is: a person with passions who is also capable of making free and responsible choices.

Surely there must be room for *that,* even in nature.

Recently, while I was wrestling with myself and "the questions," I met a writer whose books and ideas I had admired for quite some time. He had a great deal to say about the importance of intensity and spiritual-esthetic values in any society of the future, and I was quite sure that if anyone could transcend the stringencies of nature, he would be the one to do it.

One evening, after I had been listeing to him speak before a large group of people and had shared in the animated discussion which followed, he surprised me by approaching me. He suggested going for a walk. I accepted. We walked and talked . . . again animatedly . . . until finally I asked him why it was that he had come up to me.

"I am a visual and tactile person," he said.

The world went up in a series of tiny simultaneous explosions.

"Why," I thought, "why does it always have to be that way?"

I was attracted to his mind and his manner. But clearly my hopes of transcending nature had been misplaced. Where he was concerned, transcendence was secondary, nature primary. I thought of what a friend of mine had once said to me: when I was fifty years old and sagging at the seams, men would be interested in me for my mind, but until then I could expect them to be interested in me for my body. His comment made me feel a sudden strong desire to be fat and ugly and old, since no one was going to be interested in me for "the right things" while I continued to be young and attractive (not intended as vanity, but as something more closely linked to despair).

What a dilemma, I had thought then. I like being attractive, like being vital, like being sexual, like being young. But I also like to think and feel, and consider the holes in my character to be at least as crucial as the holes in my body. I don't like to be compartmentalized, with parts of me segregated off from other parts.

Of course by the time I met my "visual and tactile" companion, I had passed the stage of wishing to be fat and old and ugly. Now all I wanted was to find a good reason to stop hating men, to be able to recognize a good reason when I saw one.

His attitude didn't help any, although it was true that I had never "defined" the problem to him. It is difficult to shake hands with someone and say, "How do you do, I am a man-hater, what are you?" But it is even more difficult to overcome man-hating when in the presence of those things that helped to create it in the first place.

Nonetheless I felt deeply the *necessity* of trying. In some sense my survival seemed to depend on the effort. So despite my hostility, I kept on seeing him, talking, explaining, asking questions, trying to overcome myself and reach him at the same time, believing that a mind as sensitive as his would sooner or later be able to absorb such simple truths. But whereas his mind was extremely acute on questions concerning the needs of humanity, he seemed impossibly dense where female needs—at least mine—were concerned. I explained in terms of intensity, in terms of esthetics and in terms of humanity, using the ideas most familiar to him and most meaningful to me. But even there I encountered a stone wall. I was desirable and humanity-esthetics-intensity were peripheral.

I explained by saying that I was just a *person* and wanted to be dealt with as a person. And one day, abandoning the hope of getting across, I simply cried silently with my head on my knees. Even though he comforted me while I cried, it was not long before he reached for my body again, insisting that the communication we had been unable to achieve by talking would be achieved instead through sex.

"Sex is communication on its highest level," he said.

I agreed that it could be, but only when other means of communication had been built up first. It was, I said, trying to deal with the problem as rationally as possible, the final result of communication, a form of expression that became most meaningful when words and gestures had exhausted themselves, when the need for contact was so powerful that it transcended the possibilities for speech. It was, I said, a union of the most primitive state in which animals possessed nothing *but* touch to express their feelings, and the highest spiritual state in which language comes face to face with infinity.

"When you feel so much for a person that you can't find any words to express it . . . that's when sex really means something."

"No," he said. "You achieve that closeness *through* sex, through the joy of the physical."

For almost a week the struggle between us continued, verbal battles alternating with physical and emotional ones. Gradually I realized that this confrontation, even though it was bringing out more of my anger, hurt, and frustration, was also forcing me to come to grips with the thing for myself, forcing me to dig deep in search of meaningful answers since those answers were directly related to my immediate "fate" and not to anything abstract. The need for maintaining my own psychic balance seemed to depend on my choosing my arguments carefully enough.

I had to fight with every verbal tool I could lay my hands on, had to rummage around in the junkyard of my emotions searching for something that would redeem my insistence on refusal.

After all, I thought, if I can't make myself clear to *this* man, who, in terms of everything elese, represents the best of all possible worlds, then I can't make myself clear to anyone. He has a mind, a spirit, a body. He does not pretend to "understand" too much. He is his own person and he knows something about choices.

If I succeed, I thought, then the whole battle will have been worth it.

But if I failed?

After a few days I began to believe that I had. I finally decided to tell him to stay away and leave me alone, tell him that the cost for me was just too high, that I was reaching a stage of mental, physical, and emotional exhaustion.

It was then that I finally touched something that was real to him.

We were stretched out on the grass together. I was preparing my announcement and he was taking advantage of the silence to stroke my stomach.

"Look," I finally said, flipping over on my belly, "if I wanted you to touch my stomach, I would want to do everything else as well. But if I do I'll end up feeling empty afterward. Or else I'll hate you. And I don't want that to happen. I have a lot of experience with myself and I know that's what always happens if I'm not ready for something."

"You think *you'll* feel empty," he said, taking his hand away for a moment. "Just think how a *man* feels. He's really empty. He really loses something."

I thought about it for a while before I answered. Then I said, "Maybe that's true. But for me, for any woman, it's different. It's a different kind of emptiness. A woman doesn't lose some*thing.* She loses some*one.* The emptiness has to do with a person who was inside of you and isn't any more. If there's no way to make the transition from being full physically to being full emotionally, then the gap is just too large and the loss too great. For a woman, it's somehow much more personal if you see what I mean."

He did see and he even agreed. But a few minutes later he reached out again to touch my breast.

I pulled away. "Listen," I said, "we just finished talking about it. Can't you *try* to understand?"

He sat there for a long time without saying anything. Then finally he answered . . . but his tone was almost resigned. "I understand," he said. "I really think I do. But that doesn't change anything. Because we're both still made of flesh."

I thought about it, and knew that he was right. Flesh all of us. Flesh me. Flesh and bones and blood. Nature. Drives.

And yet . . . how much destruction could be wreaked in the name of that flesh, in the name of nature—like Christianity, whose Holy Wars took a staggering toll in human lives; for the sake of each one of nature's victories, a thousand defeats had to be suffered. Not defeats at the hands of its enemies . . . but of itself.

Was I then one of nature's casualties?

6

From strangers to friends . . . and finally to lovers and almost-lovers. From man-hating at a distance to man-hating at its closest, most real point. This is where the hatred of intimacy, or maybe the intimacy of hatred, begins. It is the starting point for all the other rages, the point where need and vulnerability are the most intense, where an experience becomes something more than that, where the possibilities for commitment and the possibilities for hatred are lined up toe to toe at the starting point.

When I was sixteen I commented to an adult that in my opinion all cynics were disappointed idealists. What I would add today is that most man-haters are probably disappointed romantics. Or at the very least, I would say, that is what I am.

For a very long time I believed that I knew a great deal about love and almost nothing about hate. Certainly I thought of men as potential sources of love, thought of myself as gentle, giving, affectionate. My life for many years centered around the expectation that sooner or later

I would find someone who would fulfill my most romantic desires, someone who would be lover, friend, confidant, companion, mentor, and advocate, someone with whom making love would be an act of transcendent beauty. Even though I had read *Madame Bovary* by the time I was twelve and had gotten the message, *Modern Screen* still had a more powerful claim on my imagination.

The old images reel through my mind: Lana Turner blending into a movie star kiss; Debbie Reynolds living happily ever after; Cary Grant performing the ultimate eroticism, slipping a hand into the back slit of a beautiful and sensual woman's dress. The Hollywood images combined with other images: Bud and Betty fumbling for each other on the front seat of *Peyton Place* cars; a prostitute in *Moulin Rouge* whose nipples were like wild strawberries; couples holding hands on the city subways; the world of Salem cigarettes; the slow, rich, floating sensuality which seemed like the movement of pure form in *Hiroshima, Mon Amour.* All together those were the things I thought of when I thought of making love and loving. The images were interspersed with images of real men, men whom I cared for in various ways (though never the right ways)—images of afternoons and nights spent in bed as if the entire world could be contained in a space of six by eight feet, always with music in the background. And if there was no radio or stereo, there was always the schmaltz my mind supplied in abundance. Percy Faith or Henry Mancini or Johnny Mathis dubbed in on top of "Us" as everyone, "Us" the universal lovers standing ten feet apart and then slowly moving into each other's arms while the music went up up up and finally blended into one crashing kiss with no noses.

That was life to me. Whether it was going to be Toulouse Lautrec (who would be transformed by love from a cripple to Prince Valiant) or Cary Grant, transformed by the presence of a woman who "really cared" after all the women who loved him for his looks, or Tony Curtis, laying down his gangland blackjack for the woman who cried out, "No no, Tony . . . no more fighting" . . . no matter who it was, in the end it was going to be "Us" . . . in the end it was going to be permanent love, permanent romance, permanent happiness . . . and maybe even a small house in the country.

So what happened? Well first of all I guess I grew up.

But even after I grew up, fragments of the old images kept sticking in my mind, making me dive into relationships as if they were clear pools of happiness which I had only to reach for and thereby attain. A man who loved me for a while once commented that I was the most vulnerable person he had ever met—which I thought was quite wonderful, since vulnerability to me then meant the capacity to be warm, receptive, and responsive. The only problem with it was that I never loved anybody for a "while." It seemed that I fell in love and that was that. When things went wrong I figured that sooner or later they would have to go right again . . . if I was patient enough. Love, I thought, was only capable of producing more love. I wasn't interested in casual intimacy anyway, and I assumed that a lot of work and a lot of caring could make up for just about anything.

For the moment, no comment about the people with whom I chose to fulfill these great expectations. Certainly I didn't make the best of all possible choices. Still, I chose from what seemed to be available . . . chose for what I thought had something to do with potential and understanding and chemistry and maturity.

I chose three times. And while I was making the choices, I did a lot of exploring. After the third time my head struck not the usual mud but a shelf of bedrock, seeming to stretch like an undiscovered vein all along the bottom edge of the pool.

After the third time I began to revise my expectations.

And new images began taking the place of the old ones, which now could be seen as if through the wrong end of a telescope, very far away, very remote. The new images were frightening. They ranged from the grotesque to the obscene to the simply horrible. Fear took the place of expectation, and hatred, staved off with resolute determination, took the place of love. I lost touch with a part of myself. Maybe it was the best part.

In the photograph I am thirteen years old. I am sitting on a wooden railing overlooking a lake. I am wearing a bathing suit. It is a movie star pose: head thrown back, chest thrust forward, one leg extended just a little bit less than the other with my right big toe touching my left ankle. Both feet are pointed. I am being sexy.

When I am not being sexy, I am trying to cope with the problem of making out. Shy boys don't ask me for dates and popular boys ask in order to make out. I have more drives than I am able to cope with . . . and am a puritan in order to make up for things. Boys do not like puritans, especially if they measure 36-24-36. Boys like me on the first date. They do not like me on the second, if there ever *is* a second. I like boys. And I don't know what to do.

I am fifteen. A boy from Harvard is home for the summer. He drives a sports car and is very handsome. He asks me for a date. My parents are thrilled. They do not know that the teenage grapevine has pegged him as a wolf. They think he is a very nice boy. So do I. I am very excited about going out with him . . . especially since we are going to a party where lots of boys from Harvard will be. Harvard is glamorous. Michael is glamorous, too. Also smart. He comes over to talk about "final arrangements" for picking me up. I have mulled over what I should do about his being a wolf, and have decided to be fair. Using formulas culled from *Facts of Life and Love for Teenagers,* I look him straight in the eye and say, "I don't drink or smoke or make out with boys I don't know . . . but if you want to take me to the party anyway, I'd love to go." I am impressed with the rhythm of the sentence, with the precise shades of meaning it conveys, with the fact that it tells him where things stand and lets him know that I like him at the same time. Exactly what the book ordered.

Except, unfortunately, I end up being impressed with myself in solitude. I spend the evening of the party at home, all dressed up and hoping against hope that *Facts of Life* will win out in the long run, that Michael will come, even if late, with renewed respect for my virtue. But Michael never shows up. *Facts of Life* is banned from the bookshelf. And my mother who said, "Even boys who want to try, will respect a girl who refuses," is judged unreliable. Not just unreliable. Through my tears I rage that she is an idiot.

I am sixteen. All boys want to do is drink beer and feel me up. I don't want to be felt up. Or rather I do, but don't want to be part of anyone's experiment. I think that I would go all the way if I liked someone enough, but boys say that girls who go all the way are sluts. I am not a slut. But when I won't let them feel me up, they say I am a prude. I can't figure out how to be myself and have boys like me. I still like boys.

I am sick of boys who won't keep their hands off me. I meet men who are much older than I am. They won't touch me. They say I'm jailbait. I don't like being jailbait, but I do like not having everyone pawing me. I meet a man who is married and about twice my age. He is a stud. He has a lot of experience and will talk with me about sex. He doesn't think girls who go to bed with men are sluts. He doesn't want to go to bed with me. He says, "Going to bed isn't everything." I agree with him, even though I think it's a lot. I decide that I am in love with him because he doesn't push me to go to bed with him.

Now I *want* to. He says no for a long time . . . for more than a year. I keep saying, "Look, being a virgin is stupid. And I don't want to do it with someone I don't love." He keeps saying that he's not the right person for it. I think that means he is being extremely considerate. It does not occur to me that maybe he doesn't love me. I think he must, even though he's never said so. Otherwise, why would he bother to keep on seeing me? It also does not occur to me that he thinks intense eighteen-year-old girls can be a handful, especially when you're married and don't want your girlfriends to interfere with your marriage. Especially when those girls make impassioned phone calls at odd hours.

After a long time I persuade him that "if I don't do it with you I'll be a virgin the rest of my life." We have already done everything else and being a *demi-vierge* is not my cup of tea. We finally do it. I feel very grown up and love him more than ever. I wait all day for him to call me to find out how I feel. I think maybe he will even send flowers. Twenty-four hours pass. Not a word from him. A week passes. Still not a word. I start to feel desperate, but I don't want to be aggressive, so I force myself not to call him. Instead, I stay in my new apartment twenty-four hours a day, call up my boss and say that I'm sick, and wait. Finally I give in to myself and call. He answers the phone and says that he has been very busy. He says he will call me back later. I wait some more. He doesn't call back.

It takes me a year to recover. I decide that I just didn't choose the right person. I start to date a lot of men . . . all kinds of men . . . the ones I meet on the street, at work, at the New School. I discover what it's like to be a single woman living alone in New York. I am nineteen.

"Just relax," the man says, the man who is Mr. Average Guy incarnate. "Why are you being so stiff?"

This is our first date. We have gone out to dinner and he has asked whether he could come up to my place for coffee. I think that's a wonderful idea. We can talk and get to know each other a little bit better.

All he wants to do is go to bed with me. I say no thank you, and he leaves. I never see him again.

"Why not?" the new man says. The new man is a professor. I think he is going to be different. "Making love is natural," he says. "I just want to mnmnmnmn."

I feel as though I am on a primitive torture rack where the test of my capacities is measured by my ability to grit my teeth and refuse to show pain. My body is strung tight from resisting. That is painful. I like making love but I don't like being pushed. "You see," I say, "I have to be in love before I want to make love." He says, "Yes yes, I understand," but won't take his hands off me. I lead him to the door and he goes home. I don't see him again.

I keep thinking that there must be someone who is interested in *me.* So I go on trying. But the trouble seems to have something to do with the fact that I'm "stacked." Men are always getting carried away at the sight of my "tits," in later years to be referred to as "boobs." "Big boobs" are thought to belong with "big cocks" and are therefore an irresistible challenge to lockerroom competitors who have been measuring the size of their penises. Every such struggle is now being tested against every girl's dormitory striptease and bra-cup comparison, and in the middle of such a crunch of myths, I seem to represent the ultimate conquest. If I'm stacked, then I must also be sexy and dying to go to bed with the biggest penis in town. Isn't it natural? The result of all this is that men who are shy virgins, or who stare in the mirror worrying about their own quarter pound of flesh become quite convinced that 36D obviously belongs with a twelve-inch extension, convinced that if I'm *that* stacked, I couldn't possibly be interested in them.

I happen to like shy men, although when they make me feel shy and I can't think of anything to say I feel scared of them and worry that I'm never going to make it as an "understanding woman." Shy men, though, are usually so scared of *me* that they stay away entirely. I also have nothing against homosexuals. I went with one to my high school junior prom because he was fun to dance with and we could really talk. Certainly *they* don't want to go to bed with me. But they seem to be scared of me too. Or even worse, contemptuous. When I am walking down the street they look at me and glare. After a while I start to think, "If they don't like me, I don't like them either."

I begin to wonder whether there are any men around at all who are worth bothering with. I seem to go out with a new batch every month. Whenever they make a pass at me, I act cold and unresponsive . . . the blank stare and passive body being my only weapons against intrusion. I have given up trying to *explain* how I feel. My earnestness always comes across as banality anyway, and usually men take advantage of my verbal concentration to relocate their hands on some potentially more fertile terrain. They seem to consider my explanations a standard resistance put up for form's sake only. Persistence, as their hands say, is the best method. Rolling over and playing dead seems to be a better defense, since nothing is so irritating to a man's pride as a woman who is (or seems to be) supremely indifferent to his expert touch. If I sit long enough without moving a muscle, giving the appearance of being utterly bored with the whole procedure, most men can be relied on to give up.

Bit by bit I start to become cynical. How can I even *think* about love if no one will go out with me more than once? Or at the most twice? I want to have a "relationship" with someone. But it seems that all my time is taken up with standing in front of my building and arguing with the man who wants to come upstairs. I see nothing wrong with his coming upstairs. But I *really* want to talk and have coffee. All he wants is more of the same thing.

Sometimes I start to get angry, but that usually provokes a paternal, "There there, what are you getting so steamed up about," followed by a renewed assault on my body. Or else I am told, "God, you're beautiful when you're angry," followed by a few more tender words and attempts to ignore the substance of my fury.

It never seems to occur to anyone that the solution to the problem might not be in more sex with less feeling, but less sex with more feeling.

I read somewhere a bit of advice offered to men who are

having difficulty with unyielding women. It is suggested that the best approach is to act shy or uninterested in sex, and that will achieve faster results than the traditional pass. I think that whoever wrote this is very smart. And now I don't trust shy men any more either.

I have reached the age of paranoia. I am only twenty-one. I think that every man alive is after a piece of ass or at least a sizable chunk of breast.

I want to make love with someone who is capable of making a real choice between abstinence and indulgence. I am drawn to men whose sexuality is as strong as my own, but I do not think it is a supreme sacrifice to get to know someone first (and deep down still think that love and sex ought to go together). I know that I am incapable of empathizing fully with the "pain" of an unsatisfied erection. But I suspect that such male suffering has been somewhat overstated for the purpose of making women feel guilty if they don't capitulate . . . suspect that self-control is no easier for me than for a man.

It seems that the only way I can get to know a man is if we work in the same office together for a long time. But everyone I ever work with is married already. I have decided I want to stay away from married men. But they're the only ones who don't come after me like gangbusters. So after several months of resistance I fall in love with my boss, who is married, thinking that "circumstances" (being married is a circumstance) are less important than the quality of the relationship itself.

Except in the long run nothing changes. Although now that I'm in love I want to go to bed again. And things have proceeded slowly enough that we do.

In some ways I make an excellent mistress. I am always waiting at the top of the stairs when he comes and I like making love in the middle of the afternoon. Except I also like to leave my apartment sometimes. It seems that we never do, because who knows when we might run into someone. Also I cannot ever call him when I need to. Also the more in love I am the more time I want to spend with him and the less I like the fact that he is married.

Things fall apart.

Now I'm really scared. I think maybe I am starting to hate men. But I also think I'm to blame for a lot of things, although I'm not sure exactly what. Well yes . . . intensity, romanticism, compulsiveness because of the fear of being ditched. Maybe what I'm most guilty of is not knowing the right men. But where are they? Who are they? I think that probably they have their own problems and are in hiding.

Finally I meet *one* man who loves *me.* But one man is not very many to choose from. And I don't happen to love him. I am very honest about it. He accepts a platonic relationship in the hope that eventually I will become ready for something else. But I am so overwhelmed by the fact that he is willing to accept me without sex, willing to go for walks with me and go to the movies and hug me, that I never get around to *wanting* sex with him. I suspect that once we get into bed everything will be ruined and we will never get *out* of bed.

In the long run I treat him badly . . . feel guilty for not

loving him and not giving him what he needs. He finally marries someone else. And I never quite forgive myself for having abused him. I conclude that I must be sick in the head from all that has happened in the past and that I can't even handle a good thing any more without destroying it. I conclude that if I hurt him, then I really can't be much good for any man. I have not yet gotten around to thinking that men by and large have not been very good to me. I just think, "That's the way men are and we have to learn to put up with it."

So I embark on another love affair, this time with a man who falls very quickly in love with me and with whom I fall in love much more slowly. By the time I am in love with him, or shortly after, he begins to fall out of love with me. During the disintegration I get into the habit of listening to my mind as if it were something that did not quite belong to me, or someone I wanted to get to know better. When I'm not listening to my mind I seem to be getting hysterical a lot. I have disaster flashes. I think that if he turns out to be "just like a man," I don't know what I'll do. Rather than think about that I think about my thoughts, and bit by bit learn to treat them as guests I'm obliged to pay attention to. They are sometimes astonishing, sometimes disgusting, sometimes abhorrent. They come to me "out of the air." I learn to recognize the signs of hostility quickly repressed, the snags in my psyche when something jams inside of it, the expressions of love that conceal expressions of hate.

I discover that I am not quite the person I thought I was.

I discover that somewhere along the line I too have become a man-hater.

We are in the shower. I look at his back, at the marks I left during the night. Nothing deep, just surface scratches. It must have been when I was past the point of being "aware." Passion is often like that. I mean I just hurt him a little bit. I soap his back trying to be gentle with the scratches, trying to soap them away. But not quite away. Because my mind is creeping up on me. My mind makes me feel proud of those scratches, makes me regard them as a seal of possession. They give me a sense of power. Even hurting him is a part of loving him, I think, and rub his back a little bit harder until he finally complains. I say I'm sorry. But I'm not.

We haven't seen each other all day. I leave the meeting early because he is going away for a week tomorrow. I wait three hours for him at the apartment. When he comes I lose my temper. He says, "I never get upset when you're late." I apologize for being upset. He says, "That's all right," his voice filled with the sweetness of victory, for now it is wholly a matter of my having been silly and not one of his having been inconsiderate. In an instant the argument is swept into oblivion, caught up in a landslide of tolerance and understanding, even though I know he will do the same thing the next time. If he hadn't *asked* me to be home early . . . but then he *always* asks and never arrives on time himself. Now though, with the mental debris cleared away (like clearing the dishes from the table by pulling the tablecloth out from under them), it is possible to make a decent transition from anger to intimacy.

"I'm exhausted," he says, putting his arms around me. "Why don't we go to bed?"

Anger flicks its red salamander tongue inside of me. I want to say no, to stay up the whole night just to make him suffer. But I would suffer more, since I am exhausted too. So we go to bed. Within two minutes he is touching me.

"Do you want to make love?" he says.

I don't answer. Part of me does and part of me doesn't. After all I still love him. Then I feel the hum rising up inside of me, slow, soft, satisfying. The part that wants to wins. I don't move away.

But suddenly, without any warning, while he is lifting and lowering himself above me, the pleasure breaks. Way way at the top, at the very best moment, I feel crushed by his weight, as if he were an oil rig ramming into my body, pumping out everything of value, or as if I am a balloon and he is crushing the air out of me. Right at the center of his orgasm I think . . . I could stop even right now, right this second. I could roll over and say, "OK, now pull out." A hysterical giggle shapes itself inside of me. That would surprise him, I think. He'll ache for the rest of the night. And at the center of my orgasm, the giggle rises to a roar.

. . .

On the surface nothing has changed, but I have become so attuned to the ways in which he expresses himself when we make love that I know when he is doing it because he needs someone, know when it is habit, know when it is affection or friendship, know when it is anger and know when it is love. Now it isn't any of those things. He is forcing himself to. The effort has a certain peremptory quality as if it were my fault for still being desirable to him when he no longer loves me. When he is finally inside of me I feel as if no one is there. I feel completely empty. If I didn't *know* that he was inside I wouldn't believe it. I realize that it's because I don't want him to reach anything inside of me if he doesn't love me.

After we stop he asks me how it was for me. He never can tell the way I can tell. I never need to ask *him.* I answer very quietly, as if providing neutral facts. "Not so good," I say. "I must have stretched out inside. You just don't fill me up any more." I can feel the pause before he answers, the rush of self-doubt that goes racing through him. I feel myself to be suddenly very powerful . . . I have the power to destroy his sense of himself just the way he destroys me. And I want to do it.

"I don't want to hurt you," I say. "But I have to tell the truth." (We have an "honest relationship," which gives me a good excuse.)

"Yes," he says. "I understand. Maybe . . ." But he doesn't finish the sentence.

The next night he can't get an erection. I'm glad but also ashamed. The thought passes through my mind that I am a castrating bitch. The thought makes me want to cry. But then I think, “Well, it serves you right,” and force myself to go to sleep.

We split up. I decide that I don’t want to have anything more to do with men. But every once in a while, I test out the water a little bit. It doesn’t require very much any more for me to recognize the signs of what’s to come. I say the hell with everything, the hell with this love and hate nonsense. I’m just going to jump into bed the way they do. No feelings, no commitments, nothing.

I manage to do it four or five times.

One morning I wake up next to a man I like, who likes me and has been wanting to go to bed with me. We went to bed.

He leaves the house. I sit in the living room for a while reading. I am having a hard time concentrating, so I put the book down and stop to listen to my thoughts again. What I hear is a string of the crudest obscenities: “up your ass mother fucker cock sucker drip drip drip” . . . everything I’ve ever heard on the streets or seen scrawled on bathroom walls. They are words I would never use, have never even heard my mind use. But there they are, invading some inner territory like armies of red ants preparing for a takeover. I listen more closely, but the unconscious voice seems to have exhausted itself from the effort of rising to that single outburst, or else perhaps it is retreating in the face of my shocked attention. All I can hear are the same words, reverberating inside my mind, more softly now, less insistently, like a sinking ship at sea slowly losing touch with its radio contact. But who on earth could the obscenities possibly refer to, I think. He didn't do anything to deserve that. Yet obviously it is directed at him.

I walk into the bathroom, take off all my clothes, and look at myself in the mirror. Suddenly I see my body slide out of focus, become fat, ugly and distorted. A surge of disgust washes over me. I feel contaminated by some crude and vulgar disease. I fill the tub with hot water and sit in it for an hour, running the hot again every time the water cools enough to reach the comfortable stage. I want to be boiled, sterilized. When I climb out of the tub, I feel better. But the string of obscenities follows me around all day until, finally, late in the afternoon, while I am walking down Fifth Avenue, someone comes up to me and whispers, "Mmm, love that cunt. Can I lick it, baby? Wanna suck my cock?" I start to run. I run all the way back to the apartment. And when I get upstairs I walk into the bathroom and throw up.

All of a sudden at the age of twenty-four I discover that I can no longer get into bed with a man. Not with any man. All of a sudden I become effectively frigid. My body is just as responsive as ever, except my mind seems to have gotten derailed. Someone touches me and I want to scream. Every once in a while I throw up or else run out of someone's apartment.

I have to say to myself, "My God, look at me. I really hate men."

. . .

That, of course, brings me right up to the present. The present consists of abstinence. I've made a couple of attempts to try again but they almost invariably result in more virulent attacks of man-hating. I shock myself almost every day now and have decided that I really am paranoid, since I can no longer distinguish sincerity from its mass-produced imitation and mistrust even those men who are not after me. I feel quite capable of being castrating and more and more often, I act as though I am. I think, "Now, how in the hell could this have happened to me?"

Sometimes the question makes me mute . . . sometimes it makes me rage. At other times I analyze it and listen to the slow time bomb ticking in my brain, waiting for it to go off.

I don't think I could make a philosophy out of man-hating. The prospect of having sex with anyone has become a source of terror in anticipation instead of the old pleasure in anticipation. And terror is not enjoyable . . . not even philosophically. But yielding to the desire for pleasure has become a trap in itself, since I can never tell how much of the brew is composed of conquest, how much of sheer physical necessity, how much of the need for power, how much of hatred. Wanting to find the point at which flesh transforms itself into spirit, I have found too often the point at which flesh seems to decompose into pure shit.

Without spirit, sex is the fastest vehicle for hatred I

know. And all too often I feel as if I am riding that train, hurtling in a direction that can only lead to an encounter with more and more demons. The same man who had once said to me, "We still are made of flesh," also admitted later that he thought I was right in asking of sex what I did. "But," he added, "it's all too rare. And men just aren't like that."

I hoped that he was wrong. I hoped that there would be ways to cut through from the worst in myself to the best . . . from the worst in others to their best. But often that hope recedes like the mirage of some miraculous bridge between humans. Often I feel myself to be stranded on the farthest shore without knowing how to get across.

Is it then the fault of men in general? Is it because of terrible incapacities in myself? Is it society?

I don't really know. Finding people to blame really helps to alter very little. It provides a degree of catharsis, but ultimately one is left with oneself, with confronting the world on the basis of what you alone possess. And if those possessions seem meager equipment in relation to "what is available out there," then some adjustment must be made. But by whom? And what kind of adjustment? Should I adjust to the "facts of life" about the nature of the male species? Should men adjust to the facts of life about women? About me?

And if neither of us can complete that adjustment, is the price we must pay an isolation so profound that real communion becomes all but impossible?

If, on the other hand, these feelings are, to a greater or

lesser degree, part of the common store of humanity, they are still not conducive to much of anything. I for one don't see myself as part of any revolutionary vanguard. I don't want to tear it all down, since I'm not too sure what it is. I don't want to help whip up a black foam of hatred in other women. Man-hating adds just one more layer of unhappiness to lives that are better off without it.

Often, though, my thoughts and feelings sit inside of me like glass eyes. I stare at them and they stare back. I think of all the theories and philosophies that are so much easier to wear than a life. I think that I am a small child in a big sandbox . . . sometimes a big child in a small sandbox. I think . . . when I get around to climbing out, I might discover the world. I might even discover that it's round.

LESBIANISM

"Refusal to make herself the object is not always what turns woman to homosexuality; most lesbians on the contrary, seek to cultivate the treasures of their femininity. . . . Between women love is contemplative; caresses are intended less to gain possession of the other than gradually to re-create the self through her; separateness is abolished, there is no struggle, no victory, no defeat; in exact reciprocity each is at once subject and object, sovereign and slave; duality becomes mutuality."

SIMONE DE BEAUVOIR, *The Second Sex*

" 'What does a woman see in a woman that she can't see in a man?' Doctor Nolan paused. Then she said, 'Tenderness.' "

SYLVIA PLATH, *The Bell Jar*

1

I don't really know what a lesbian is. When I was ten years old, I thought I knew. That was the year I stole a copy of *The Well of Loneliness* from the revolving bookshelves in Whelan's corner drugstore because I was afraid that if I paid for it at the counter, the storeowner, who had known me since I was six, would arrest me for perversion. Lesbianism was "that awful thing" women did together, although at the time (and until very recently) I couldn't quite get my highly visual imagination to focus on precisely what "that awful thing" was. What I could do, though, was understand the words on book jackets. *The Well of Loneliness* cost thirty-five cents. The cover read, "Denounced, banned and applauded—the strange love story of a girl who stood midway between the sexes." The back cover started off with large blue letters asking, "Why can't I be normal?" Even though the rest of the blurb said that the book was "frank and sincere" it was the "why can't I be normal" that seized the eye . . . and the imagination.

The book was not to be read at home, but in the park. It was a secret book, for my parents, who were as remote from vulgarity as I was from propriety, thought that "sex books" and "sex talk" were highly uncivilized. Sex was a very private matter to be talked about seriously or not at all. It was a "sacred subject." *Into the World,* a story about dogs and cats and horses and finally a mama, giving birth, was a proper introduction to sex. It was given to me when I was eight. *The Well of Loneliness,* however, was an improper introduction, lesbianism being by definition barred from all aspirations to sacredness.

Even though I read *Into the World* and was interested in it, I still lacked sexual reverence. Unlike my parents, sex talk made me giggle, especially when I was with girls my own age who talked incessantly about things like "cherry-popping." In addition, I was still polymorphously perverse, attracted to everything and everyone, including horses, dogs, my canary Timothy, whom I often cradled between my nonexistent breasts, trees (particularly the cherry trees on Riverside Drive, which had trunks ideal for climbing on and dangling from), my father, my best friend's father, and finally, my best friend herself, who was just as "perverse" as I.

By the time I was ten, Lisa and I had developed a game which we played whenever we were together. It was a "touch game" which really required going to bed together. This was conveniently arranged by setting up sleepover dates at one another's houses, dates on which we pleaded to sleep together in order to talk after the lights were out. After our parents had knocked on the door at least three or four times, telling us to be quiet (we disobeyed the order deliberately, not wanting to seem too obedient and cause suspicion), we got down to the really important business of the evening. We lay there with our arms around each other, kissing each other's flat chests, turned upside down to nuzzle at each other, used our tongues, and even went so far as to imitate the dogs we had seen on the street by crawling around and around the bed sniffing one another. We giggled a great deal in between our exploits, half from nervousness and half from sheer sensual pleasure. Then deep in the darkness, we murmured dirty jokes in one another's ears . . . relishing especially the one about the Exploring Fly which was so graphic that it never ceased to inspire us.

Lisa and I, of course, had no "ideas" about what we were doing. We knew, though, that it would be bad if we were caught. We considered grownups to be too proper for such things and expected that they would never understand how fine it was to lie together feeling such intense and joyous animal pleasure from touching one another. If, in all likelihood, they would think we were terrible, then the only solution was not to let them know, to protect their innocence and make sure that we would have the freedom to continue our explorations. (It is in this way, I suppose, that parents and children mutually reinforce the myths about each other's naivete, which can never be substantiated, since neither ever dares to raise the questions that would shatter forever the dimly romanticized aura that surrounds the other, and preserves the desired distance between them.)

I certainly had never stopped doing anything because I was told it was bad. But if I had actually been caught fooling around with Lisa I am sure I would have cried for shame, not over the act itself, but over the violation of my world which discovery implied, since what I really felt I had to protect were my sense perceptions against the onslaught of values that were denied by everything I had experienced. Those values, however, were extraordinarily insidious, so that even as I was denying that I cared what my parents thought, I soon started having nightmarish fantasies about becoming sterile for the rest of my life as a result of what I considered to be my "perversion." In my dreams, I was constantly being tortured and tossed into pits. I was a lesbian, I thought. The most terrible thing one could possibly be. Being a lesbian meant one thing to me . . . not doing what we had done, but having people look at you as if you had just decided to shit in the middle of their expensive living room rug. Lesbianism was not what one did; it was what people thought about what one did. And that was bad. Very bad. Not only bad . . . it was disgusting.

"Enlightened" parents, of course, would protest against my exaggerated sense of my own lesbianism. They would insist to me that, childish sexuality being what it is, my lesbianism was merely part of a phase that all little girls go through.

For me, at the time, the word "phase" had absolutely no meaning though. There was only the present. And I felt, somehow, every time my mother came into the room where Lisa and I were sleeping together, that the word "phase" had no real meaning to her either. Wanting badly to succeed as a post-Freudian, progressive parent, she was nonetheless afflicted with a hidden and persistent terror. She was a mother before being a post-Freudian, and her instincts, as always, were more powerful than her intellectual tolerance. What I felt, beyond that tolerance, was the depth of her fear. What were we doing, she must have thought? And what should she do? Should she warn us about not going too far? Should she bring up subjects that might not even have entered our minds? Should she ignore us and "it"? Should she pretend she hadn't noticed that anything was happening? Should she separate us and deflect our "natural" development? Her state of profound uncertainty, her insecurity, her doubt, her sense of moral ambiguity were what affected me the most deeply. They were real in a way that her textbook knowledge was never real; as they must be real to all children who are dependent upon their perceptions and know nothing about fancy intellectual awarenesses, who know, finally, only what they can see and feel.

My mother. The idea of having a premarital affair would have strained her inner resources beyond their natural capacities. How then could she possibly accept the idea of her own daughter having a homosexual experience at the age of ten, even if the "authorities" told her it was normal? My father, concerned as he was with the question of whether or not a woman ought to be a virgin when she married—how could he accept it?

Of course, if the experience were described to them through an intermediary, it might be easier. If someone discussed the issue of "childhood explorations of one's own sexuality" at a parents' meeting, their ambivalence, the trap of insight mingled with terror, might be avoided. The "issue" would then be medically-psychologically sanctioned, stamped with the Good Housekeeping Seal of Approval. But what about when they came home again? And it was their daughter? What about when the language changed? When the reality was that their daughter and her friend were enthusiastically using their tongues on each other's clitorises?

Then the words weren't safe any more. Then it was no longer a part of conceptual life. Then it was charged with the kind of immediacy that makes real life so much more filled with a sense of authentic taboo than conceptual life ever could be.

From the beginning of my "affair" with Lisa, I sensed those contradictions. On the one hand, I was having a "love affair," which to my own immediate perceptions was morally neutral, an expression of simple, natural pleasure. On the other hand, my island of sexual indulgence was ringed by mountains of guilt. So long as I remained in that little island world, alone with Lisa, everything was all right. But if I tried to climb out? If I ventured among the grownups, among the winding mazes of their minds?

Obscurely, I felt the weight of that intellectual schizophrenia that surrounded me. Obscurely, I became a part of it.

. . .

One night, after Lisa's and my exploits had been going on for about a year, my parents went to visit some friends overnight. Lisa and I were left alone together. We persuaded my parents to allow us to sleep in their room, and went to bed disgracefully early. That night the two of us had a veritable orgy. There was enough room in that bed for an army of little girls, all giggling ferociously, all caught up in their own delicious sense of collective adventure. We spent hours trying out new things, freed for the night from the specter of parental shock and guilt. Free, finally, to just *be.*

We were so free, in fact, and so absorbed in our mutual pleasure, that we never even heard the front door open. My parents, trying to be considerate, kept their voices down to whispers, and when they opened their bedroom door, they did it as quietly as possible. I have never in my life, I think, been as thoroughly shaken as I was at that moment. My entire world of amoral fervor was split in two, divided by a stroke of moral lightning. Only seconds before the door had opened, I was on top of Lisa, and we were pounding up and down like a team of horses sweating through the last laps of a race. I had just rolled off her, and was stretched out prone next to her. At that moment, despite my terror of discovery, some ancient reflex of survival remained with me, and I found myself snoring loudly, as if to drown out the sound of my heart pounding. Exactly when did they open the door, I thought, in between heavily accented snores? Was it before I climbed off Lisa or after? Did they know what we had been doing?

Had they seen? Were we going to be drawn and quartered or sent to an insane asylum? Would we be disowned or beaten or disgraced for life? Would we ever be able to face anyone again?

There was, of course, no way to find out the answers and as my parents stood in the doorway of their bedroom, I went through elaborate though numbed pretensions of having just been awakened from a deep sleep, acting as though I was too drowsy to even say hello. I was so frightened it didn't even occur to me to wonder why they had come home early. But neither of them said a word. They just stood there, looking at us, and then closed the door and went out.

I remember nothing of what happened the following morning. I don't even remember whether or not they were home when we woke up. All I remember is my sense of absolute doom. For days after the door opened, I was convinced that every time my mother looked at me, she was seeing a monster she could hardly bear to call her own. I couldn't even bring myself to look at her. The thought of her knowledge, which was never made explicit, haunted me for months afterward, haunted me well into the summer when the whole family went to the country. It was only then that I purged myself of my guilt . . . or rather, purged myself of one kind of guilt, and took on another kind. That summer I betrayed Lisa—and myself.

I didn't know what else to do. I hardly felt able to take on the responsibility of the whole business myself, and gradually, as the summer progressed, it became more and more clear to me that even if my mother had not actually seen me doing something, she still knew. She knew because she was my mother, and she always knew everything. She knew because I was ashamed now, as I never had been before, knew because I hadn't put on a good enough act, or because of other times, or because she had tiny electrodes screwed into my brain connecting it with hers, electrodes that told her instantly when something was wrong, even told her what it was. She knew because . . . well, because I *believed* she knew. And that, finally, was enough.

So one day when she and I were having a heart to heart talk, I "confessed." I came clean. I talked about my friendship with Lisa and said, "You know, mother, I'm worried about her. I have a feeling she's a lesbian." I could have shot myself the minute I said the words, shot myself for the queer feeling of relief that came over me, the queer sense of vengeance. It was, after all, Lisa's fault, I thought. If she hadn't wanted to do it, then I wouldn't have done it. But deep down I felt as if the soul had been scorched out of me forever, as if, with the lie, with the betrayal of our intimacy, I had shattered forever my own child's world, shattered my belief in my own perceptions . . . had given up, surrendered to the grownups.

My mother just looked at me for a few moments without speaking.

Then she said, "Well, I had an idea it was something like that." And no more.

The subject was never mentioned again. But that was the end of Lisa's and my friendship.

And from then until now I have always had enormous difficulty imagining what it is that two women *do* with each other.

As far as I was concerned, my "fate" was settled. I was irrevocably guilty, guilty of something, although that something was never precisely defined. It was clear to me by this time that being a lesbian was synonymous with being evil. And even though I never again acted with the same simplicity and directness as I had with Lisa, some stubborn belief lodged itself inside of me that I was to be eternally in cahoots with all those women whose faces were pressed close together on the covers of paperbacks that screamed out, "Their Illicit Love Life Shocked Everyone . . . Even the Man Who Thought They Both Loved *Him!*" That, of course, was the standard paperback presentation of lesbianism and since I was exposed to no other, I assumed it was the correct one.

I had as yet no definite sense of masculinity or femininity to further complicate my understanding of what a lesbian was supposed to be, so I doubt it would have occurred to me to think that I was acting out a masculine role by being on top of Lisa instead of the other way around. What I *had* felt was that something was to be gained by making myself seem like the "passive participant" in our alliance, rather than admitting that I was the instigator and aggressor. Being the reluctant partner in a childish liaison was quite different, as I understood it, from being the one whose mind had to be fumigated, squeezed dry, quarantined, or lobotomized for attempting to seduce a "mere child," even if I was a child myself.

I was a tomboy, yes, but I never thought to associate *that* with what I had done. I had been doused throughout my childhood with a million rules and regulations about how to act if I wanted to be "feminine," but I had no ideas of my own about what being feminine was, and when my father said to me—as I was on the way to a party for which I had reluctantly dressed up—that if I wanted to be popular I had to make a choice between being a baseball player and being a girl, I answered that I intended to be both. I emphasized *both* by pounding my fist into the baseball mitt which I had decided to bring along with me at the last moment.

So I made no connection between being a lesbian and being a "dyke." At that stage of my life I had as yet no theory of personality for lesbians. How could I have, since as far as I could tell, the only important things about Lisa's and my adventures were that we had touched each other, had been thrilled by it, and were both female. If I saw myself as a grotesque at times, it was as a *moral* grotesque, and not as a personality grotesque.

In fact, I would say that the experience with Lisa probably made it difficult for me to *ever* form a consistent theory of personality for lesbians, and so I assumed that there were as many different kinds of lesbians as there were kinds of people. For if Lisa and I could be lesbians, then anyone could be a lesbian, and anyone, by some terrible twist of fate, could be "bad." Certainly Lisa and I didn't fit any of the popular lesbian typecastings. We didn't hate boys (except when they deserved to be hated); we didn't act or talk tough; we wanted to get married and have babies; and we looked very much like what we were: averagely androgynous ten-year-old girls. We both took ballet lessons, sang in the Sunday school choir (she was a soprano and I was an alto—ah, alto, well perhaps that . . .), fell in love with a new boy every week and fantasized together about grownup sex (male-female style). I was wild and undisciplined (if those can be considered "masculine" traits), but even as a tomboy, when I watched the Miss America pageant on television I burned to grow up and be "her," the beloved of the entire country.

If I had thought that what I did with Lisa would keep me out of the running for Miss America forever, I would have been even more shocked than I was at the thought of insane asylums. Insane asylums were part of my nightmares; Miss America was part of my dreams. And I did not think that my dreams could be threatened by *anything*, let alone what Lisa and I did. Little did I know that even the taint of tomboydom was sufficient to send the good judges scurrying in search of shelter, or that my dreams would one day become the target of a lot of angry women who had once perhaps had the same dream, and were furious at how it had betrayed them (and me as well), had betrayed all of us who thought of ourselves as "All-American."

Lisa and I were, I suppose, what are called "latent" lesbians. We were also potential, or latent, rebels, baseball players, organic farmers, thieves, storytellers, freaks, voyeurs, geniuses, burlesque queens, automobile casualties, deep-sea divers, daydreamers, failures, and imitators. We were potentially everything that came into our overripe imaginations, and much that did not—except that this *particular* potential never seemed, to me at least, to be subject to alteration. It was like running to the sea with a forest fire cutting off your return path, running and running until you would finally be forced to plunge in, regardless of whether you had ever learned to swim or not. Being a lesbian was, to my melodramatic mind, the way of death.

Naturally ideas like that are going to make you allergic to whatever it was you had a potential for in the first place, and as a result you will probably never be sure whether that potential wasn't realized because you repressed it with a violence equivalent to your fear, or whether it would have simply withered away of its own accord. You never know which you really are: a latent lesbian or a latent heterosexual. And since it may be years, as it was in my case, between your first full sexual experience with a member of your own sex, and your first full sexual experience with the opposite sex, it is easy to be tortured by the thought that *perhaps,* when the moment you dreamed about with a man would actually come true . . . you would *then* discover that you were, after all, a lesbian and nothing else.

That, of course, was my real fear, and for the next couple of years after the episode with Lisa, my inner life was sprinkled with anxiety about the future, my doubts consolidating themselves every time I picked up a book containing references to "those women."

By the time I was twelve, a persistent part of me was beginning to surrender to the invidious belief that if I were a lesbian, then I had to be like the stereotype, whether I was aware of it or not. Often, when I would look into a mirror, I would simply stop seeing me altogether and start seeing a lesbian—despite my knowledge that the stereotype had nothing to do with what I was really like. After a year or two of teeter-tottering between the image and the reality, I began to have a rather schizophrenic sense of identity, and soon came to doubt my perceptions altogether.

The confusions about what a lesbian was and whether or not I was one waxed and waned according to the immediate circumstances of my life. At the times when a boy liked me, I assumed that I must be all right. When a boy didn't, I was inclined to wonder whether it was because I was obviously marked in some way. Since I was tall, somewhat aggressive (although socially shy), intellectually precocious, and a tomboy, there were not very many boys who swooned at my feet, so the specter of lesbianism had plenty of space in which to maneuver. "Femininity" when you are twelve is extremely important. And by any of the standard criteria, I just wasn't feminine.

It didn't matter any more that I was boy-crazy, that I felt sexy dancing close or had fantasies about doing it in the back seat of a car with those charged words, which always seemed to describe the female anatomy and not the male (whom did I identify with, the boy who was doing the touching, the girl who was being touched . . . or both?)—all the descriptions ringing in my ears until I could hardly sleep at night. The only fact that counted at those times when there wasn't a boy around to anchor my sense of female identity was that my first sustained sexual experience had been with a girl. And not only that, but my first authentic experience combining sex with expressive tenderness, warmth, humor, affection, shared interests and enthusiasms, equal strengths and weaknesses, had *also* been with a girl. And boys, whether they knew it or not, would have to contend with that as much as anything else.

I was not conscious of making such comparisons or setting such standards. I did not think that my first sexual experience was bound to serve as a subconscious model for what sexual experiences with anyone, male or female, ought to be like. In fact, it didn't even occur to me that it was possible to expect that kind of closeness with a boy. What one shared with a boy was . . .

Well, what was it? I never thought about that. Nor, probably, did any of the other girls. We just took it for granted. All of us had an available model (in addition to our parents) for our relationships with the opposite sex. That model was based on our relationships with our own sex. And yet none of us made use of such a model. Instead, we depended upon an entirely new one, as if the gap between boys and girls was so great that nothing in our past experience could be applied to it.

Boys, we said, were the ones who really counted. Girls

were "just friends" and therefore to be put in second place as supplements to our concern with boys. The result of that, given the nature of those early adolescent boy-girl contacts, was that friendships, particularly sexual friendships, were automatically devaluated, and sex, even if it was devoid of tenderness, devoid of an understanding we would have *demanded* from our friendships, was acclaimed the champ. The process that had been affirmed in our friendships—closensess first and sex growing out of it—was reversed. If friendship entered into our relationships with boys, it was by a freak chance. Sex brought us together. And closeness was extraneous.

Was that an inevitable part of growing up? Was it natural for us to throw overboard all our ways of thinking and being for the sake of sex? Certainly I wasn't immune to the popular sexual obsessions, and I too developed crushes on boys who would never have won merit badges for their characters. I assumed that boys just couldn't or wouldn't understand anything that went deeper than a giggle. And they assumed that we understood nothing *but* giggling. Was that because we were so radically different from each other? Was the gulf that existed between us (a gulf that could only be bridged by our mutual sex drives) so great that friendships between us were impossible? Or was it more a question of our really being very much alike, equally trapped in roles and self-images that would not allow us to treat each other as human beings? Were we afraid, finally, of revealing precisely those things that made us similar at a time when everything seemed to hang on "acting like a man" or "acting like a woman"? Of course, one cannot force kids (or adults for that matter) to feel things they don't feel, or not to feel the things they do. But it is almost impossible to know what is "natural" for kids to feel, impossible to know what is the result of conditioning. And, as much as I think a certain awkwardness is "natural" between the sexes (perhaps throughout one's entire life), I am nonetheless reasonably sure that our attempts to behave like grownup men and women represented radical falsifications of ourselves, forcing us to act in ways that were anything but natural.

Life with boys was an endless round of pretenses. There was almost nothing you could share, or hope for, or expect from them, outside of an extraordinarily powerful chemistry. At that stage, however, I didn't bother to compare what one shared with boys and what one shared with girls. The only thing I cared about was the fact that all my dreams focused on boys. And yet, what actually happened with boys was always so miserably unsatisfying, so remote from my dreams, so narrow and petty that . . . well, I didn't know. All I knew was that, never having dreamed of loving a girl, I had in fact already done it. *That* was scary.

The problem was that, observed from a distance, boys were interesting people who did all of the things that I liked to do. It was just when you tried to enter into each other's worlds that everything changed. They were no longer real and it was impossible to be real with them. They thought it was unfeminine to play baseball, but they would allow you on the team if you promised to hit a homerun every time (I homerunned one out of every three times at bat, and the other two I swung on behalf of the rest of humanity and struck out). Once you were on the team you were automatically not quite a girl, except for the fact that you were expected to hit homeruns or quit. Consequently, I was in a constant state of anxiety about living up to the boys' standards—standards they would never have set for themselves. And since there were not enough female baseball players to make a team, I and the other stalwarts in my class submitted to the glowering judgments.

Off the baseball field, the problems with boys were more complex. At least when they were involved in team sports, boys yelled and cursed and laughed and fumed. If they were mad at you for striking out they told you to shape up or ship out. But off the field they became phonies, suckers for the phoniness of "real girls." They succumbed in droves to Judy Silver's giggles and helplessness, utterly ignoring those of us who were on their team, those of us who knew them when they were most themselves. Most of the girls, suitably impressed by the effect that Judy's giggles had on the boys at our school, tried hard to imitate her, while others, like myself, rebelled, calling her an idiot, meanwhile wishing that we could have the idiot's successes.

No girl would think of acting helpless in front of another girl. Most of us assumed automatically that with boys it was necessary to *act,* while with girls, at least the girls you were friendly with, it was necessary to *be,* even if "being" sometimes meant being ridiculous.

In the classroom, of course, the problem was accentuated even more. Boys were invariably scared of girls who were just as smart or smarter than they were. If you wanted boys to like you, you had to choose between fulfilling your expectations of yourself as well as your teacher's expectations of you, or fulfilling the expectations the boys had. Since the teachers stopped being a part of your world as soon as the bell rang, the boys' values usually won out. In my case, they didn't, since despite the disastrous consequences, I never could resist mental acrobatics.

With girls, though, such problems didn't even exist. There were popular girls and unpopular girls. You were automatically popular if boys liked you. It didn't matter what other girls thought. It didn't matter whether you were smart or dumb. This fact, although constricting in many respects, conferred a relative freedom on the relationships which could exist *between* girls, since what you did with a girl never counted as much. It was always possible to find girls who were just as smart as you were, or smarter, or else girls who just didn't much care about your mental status, girls who entered enthusiastically into the competition, banged you royally on the head with verbal clubs in the classroom, and then compounded the injury later on by cracking you in the shins with their hockey sticks. If girls could battle to win and could be crushed in defeat, no matter what happened, they would never consider you *inferior* if you won. Whereas boys automatically considered you inferior whether you won or lost, but especially if you won.

On the less competitive side of the ledger, there was the matter of simple affection. You could put your arms around a girl at school or hold hands with her in the halls. Everyone knew that that meant you were best friends. With a boy, though, especially with a boy in the seventh or eighth grade, you made sure to kiss each other in the dark and avoid each other in the halls.

With a girl, you could talk about your fears, your hopes, your expectations, and your defeats, knowing that telling her about all of those things did not mean risking the loss of her friendship. But with a boy you always had to balance precariously between trying not to tell him about too many successes (lest he think you too good for him) and not telling him about too many defeats (lest he think you not good enough). As for your dreams, since they usually concerned him, it was best not to confide them at all, since he would either mock them, be frightened of them, or else think that they were "just like a girl."

There was really not very much that you could realistically share with a boy . . . except for that crazy pounding in the head you felt whenever a boy you liked passed you in the hall.

And that . . . well, that was very important. At least I thought it was.

Every once in a while though, long after my friendship with Lisa was over, I would have wishful flashes, flashes that perhaps one day I would meet a boy, the right boy, who would be to me what Lisa had been: friend, lover, cohort, companion, and confidante. But when I thought of Lisa herself, thought of that abortive night in my parents' bedroom, I shuddered with disgust . . . shuddered and thought, "Oh Lisa—ugh."

2

For several years after that, the "lesbian problem" disappeared. Boys occupied more and more of my thoughts, and it was not long before I forgot about Lisa completely, or at least relegated her to some subterranean chamber of my memory where she was unlikely to do further damage to my self-image. By then I was going to a private progressive school where boys and girls were encouraged to mix, and I was deeply absorbed in learning how. Mixing usually boiled down to having parties where everyone necked with the lights off, and invariably I was torn between my fascination with my own body, its strange leaps of eroticism, and my awkward embarrassment over the fact that we all seemed to be doing the same things, imitating and watching each other, settling down to the necking business as if our ruptures of feeling could be trimmed down to assembly line sizes and shapes.

But suddenly, at the end of the ninth grade school year, the whole pattern of my life changed. My family moved to a small mill town in western Pennsylvania, and I, with my adolescent roots hanging out like raw ganglia, moved with them. I was fifteen that summer, and it took me no time at all to make the discovery that the local high school boys were far less smooth than the boys I'd known in private school, far less inclined to the gradualism of group seductions. I didn't care about etiquette and technique terribly much. But I did care about being approached at beach parties by lumbering creatures with adolescent beer bellies who came reeling across the sand and suddenly, without even saying hello, clamped wet, foul-smelling mouths on top of mine, guzzling at me as though I were just another variety of brew.

After a few weeks of trying to adapt to such slices of Americana, I started looking for new ways to use up my energy, afraid that if I didn't do something with it, I would ruin my life by turning into a compulsive masturbator.

What I found to replace the local beach parties was the local summer stock theater. Watching the shows go into production, I was mesmerized by the atmosphere of casual intimacy, glamour, and hard work that permeated the place, and after a week of hanging around, I asked the director if I could work as an apprentice. I lied and said I was eighteen. He believed me, so I was taken on and assigned to props.

That first evening I raced home with the news and was greeted with a blast of parental fury. "The theater," my father yelled. "No daughter of mine is going to work in any theater."

I yelled back that I was going to work there no matter

what he thought, and he said that if I did he was never going to speak to me again.

For the rest of the summer he didn't speak to me. Actresses and prostitutes, as far as he was concerned, all belonged in the same category, so my mother, acting as mediator, spent most of her time relaying vital messages back and forth. "The poor child has nothing to do with herself up here," my mother said.

"Then let her do nothing," he answered, and went back to his silence.

After two weeks of shuttling back and forth between the dramatic freedom of the theater and the cramped tensions of home, I finally met Rona. Rona was about forty years old and seemed to be made of solid platinum: platinum hair, platinum skin, platinum voice. She was drunk a good deal of the time, was constantly surrounded by people, and told outrageous jokes. She had the beginning of a midriff bulge and greedy, erotic eyes, like the eyes of a Siamese cat that has spent its life foraging in the garbage cans of greasy spoons, but still knows itself to be a Siamese. When Rona wasn't laughing, her silence was louder than her voice, and there was an odor of disintegration and waste about her, as if she were rusting away from the inside, as if the rust was just about to crack through the surface of her skin.

I fell madly and impulsively in love with her. It was not so much because she was strangely glamorous (everyone in the theater was), but because I felt obscurely that she possessed a kind of defeated and therefore reckless courage. I was convinced that deep down she was lonely, and, like all the alcoholic artists and writers I'd read about, was afraid of the dark.

Within three days after I'd met her, I began to cling to her like a sea anemone, sucking up every ounce of emotional energy she gave off. I watched her from the sidelines when she was the center of a group, watched her play the comedienne, and my sentimental bias reinterpreted everything she said or did as a sign that she was a woman suffering in silence. I admired and identified with that. I thought if you were going to be great, you had to suffer greatly, in the grand style, without being a martyr, but defiantly . . . even if it cost you everything.

I became Rona's companion. It flattered her ego to be surrounded by such constant adulation, and flattered mine that she allowed me to spend time with her. I wanted her to know that I knew what she was really like, but there didn't seem to be any way of telling her without upsetting that balance of pride and control which enabled her to function, so I settled instead for outright adulation. Often, when we were talking, incoherent waves of tenderness and sympathy would come rushing out of me, and if she even looked at me with warmth, I wanted to reciprocate the attention by handing her a rare tropical fruit or a stone that was a million years old, wanted to carve out the lines in my palm and give them to her, wanted to become the audience in the theater cheering itself hoarse with adoration. I wanted to take care of her . . . and to be taken care of.

Three weeks later I decided to run away from home. My

mother had gone to the city for two days, leaving me in the uneasy company of my father, who still wasn't speaking to me. On the first evening alone with him, war broke out between us when I announced that I was going to a cast party after the performance. In no time at all we were hurling accusations back and forth, vying for control of lives that long ago had outstripped our capacities to comprehend them. He thundered that he didn't care if I had special problems. Theater people were too corrupt and too old for me and I would go to the performance over his dead body. I yelled that he was immature and ought to be glad I was so involved in something constructive instead of making me feel I ought to die of shame. He said that I didn't have to die of shame, but that his word was final. Then he walked over to his rocking chair and started to rock. He rocked as if he wanted to push his way clear across the crumbling cultural edifices of an entire continent, to return to a world where things made sense, where children listened to their parents instead of the other way around, where fathers were the established heads of the family and daughters were chaperoned. He rocked, and I stormed off.

Five hours later, after thinking it over in the privacy of my bedroom, I left the house. Since I thought of everything in terms of absolutes, running away was a matter of permanent consequences. I plotted out my life and decided that I wanted to spend it with Rona.

Within half an hour I was curled up in Rona's bed, surrounded by bottles of Dewar's scotch, pots of mascara, splashes of powder, tubes of lipstick, boxes of tissues, boxes of pills, a clock set on its side, a dozen photographs of her tacked on walls and strewn across tables and chairs, and a diaphragm in an open case next to the bed, alongside a photograph of her first husband (there had been five). Surrounded . . . but without Rona, since she was still at the cast party.

Waiting for her, I fell asleep with the lights on. It was late when she came in, with a stud named Jim, who was closer to my age than hers.

"Hi," I said, sitting up in bed. "I ran away from home."

"For Christ's sake, what did you do *that* for," she said, her face tightening with annoyance. "Do you want to get me arrested or something?"

I couldn't understand what she could possibly be arrested for, but I could understand that she was angry, angry enough to want me out of there. Not knowing whom to blame, I decided that it was all Jim's fault. He was trying to take Rona away from me. When Rona asked him to leave I had a childish desire to stick my tongue out at him as he went through the door.

As soon as he was gone, Rona came over to the bed, sat down and put her arms around me. "You shouldn't have done that, baby," she said softly, her voice stripped now of that harsh, rasping quality which had terrified me a few moments ago. "It was a mistake, a bad mistake." I could smell the mixture of stale sweat and oversweet perfume, along with the scotch she had been drinking, but somehow the sickliness of it made her all the more beautiful to me.

Then she kissed me and held my head against her breasts. Out of some faraway corner of my mind, the image of Lisa and me touching each other slipped slowly into focus. Superimposed upon it was another image, of a line drawing I had seen as a child in a medical text, illustrating the process of breast feeding. The drawing had mesmerized me then, and the thought of it now mesmerized me again. I felt transformed: I was simultaneously Rona's mother and her child, her lover and her guardian. There was a longing in me for something old, childlike, and never satisfied. But the word "lesbian" kept ringing in my ears, a word that was real to me and yet completely remote from the welter of needs and feelings that had suddenly taken over my consciousness. I wanted to stay with Rona forever.

She held me that way for several minutes, rubbing the back of my neck very gently, while my body grew simultaneously taut with resistance and weak with acquiescence.

I think if at that point she had not said "Let's go now," if she had instead begun to make love to me, I would have done it, carried along by the intensity of my feelings. But she didn't make love to me; she said, "Let's go."

I cried and insisted that I didn't want to, that I didn't have any home.

She smiled and said I did. Then she kissed me again, a kiss that erased all the boundaries between passion and affection. When she brought me back to the house, she woke my father up. He tried very hard to be courteous to her, but I could tell he was noticing how drunk she was, thinking that she was a bad influence, and conscious that his authority had once again been defied—not only defied, but disputed before a stranger.

The following day when I went to work, a friend of mine told me that word had reached the theatrical grapevine: I was having an affair with Rona. He wanted to know if it was true. I said no, but I didn't believe myself. I believed that even if it wasn't true, it could just as well have been. That was what counted. But I was so ashamed of being "discovered," felt so guilty and so certain that I had been condemned by everyone around me, that I disappeared from the theater the same afternoon, and spent most of the next three days walking alone in the woods, afraid to face anyone, afraid to tell my father, afraid most of all to confront Rona ever again. The more I thought about it, the worse things seemed. Even though no one had actually judged me, I felt judged. I thought I was unfit for the world. I thought I was grotesque. For the rest of the summer I didn't go back to the theater. I gave no explanation to my parents, except that I had decided there were other things I wanted to do. My father often looked at me, as if waiting for me to talk, and his face reflected all of his conflicting impulses: his vulnerability, his love, his hidden desire to reach me. Stronger than all of those, though, was his stubborn pride, which canceled out any possibility for communication. So we looked at each other and were silent.

Shortly afterward, I met a woman and her husband while on a trip to New York. I was attracted first of all to her, and then to him, but by then I was so frightened of being attracted to a woman, so overcome by a sense of infinite consequences, that I ignored my feelings for her, and focused exclusively on him. He was twice as old as I was, very experienced, very wise in the ways of the world. Eventually I talked to him about Rona. He dismissed the attachment as insignificant. I hid my astonishment mostly because I wanted so badly to believe him. The way in which I tried the hardest to believe him was by falling in love. That was how my first affair began.

Probably the entire episode with Rona would have seemed much less crucial in retrospect if it hadn't triggered such a rash of responses and determined in many ways the pattern of my life for years to come. I was already so steeped in trying to comprehend the meanings of things that very little found its way through the filter of my imagination without being elaborated and dissected, considered from this angle or that, interpreted and investigated. Everything was food for the grist mill, everything the starting point for something else. I became obsessed with trying to sort out the contradictions in my own responses. But the interpretations, like Chinese boxes, seemed endless, all of them equally plausible. It was so easy for me to imagine what *might* have happened, to believe in the possibilities as much as I believed in what actually *did* happen. It was enough for me to know that I had responded passionately to Rona. I was unable to distinguish one kind of passion from another. All I knew was that I loved her and would have (or so I thought) done anything to be close to her. What terrified me about the theater gossip was not so much that other people thought Rona and I were lesbians, but that *I* believed it was true. I couldn't tell for sure whether I had grown attached to Rona out of sympathy and affection, out of the heartfelt warmth that can so easily transform itself into a passion . . . or whether all the rest, the sympathy, the warmth and affection, had been latecomers on the scene, developed as a consequence of that "perverted" sexuality I had been determined to repress. Nor could I tell whether my first affair with a man was the product of an authentic love or a substitute passion. I didn't know whether I had become attracted to him because he was attractive in his own right, because his wife was beautiful and I was afraid of being attracted to her, or because he had managed to cast a long enough shadow over the figure of Rona that my faith in my own normality was temporarily restored. I never knew finally what was compensating for what, or if there were any compensations at all. I felt as if a kind of moral vacuum had opened up inside of me so that every time I examined my motives, my impulses, and their connection to what I believed was right, I found myself in a country of the spirit that seemed to disintegrate the moment I touched it. Loving, as I understood it, was good, but loving a woman was bad. Or maybe just certain ways of loving women were bad. Which ways though? How did one distinguish passionate sympathy from sexual love? How fit oneself into the notion of "adolescent crushes" when nothing else about my life seemed to be adolescent? I thought I was a grownup and subject to grownup laws of behavior. It seemed to me that, maybe, according to those grownup laws, my love for Rona only became *really* bad if I went to bed with her. If that was true, then it was not loving a woman that was wrong, it was going to bed with her. I hadn't gone to bed with Rona, but there was no reason why I couldn't have. The lines between feeling and doing were terribly obscure to me, even though I sensed they were crucial. Feeling, to me, was the same as doing: my imagination made it so.

Still, I would have done anything to avoid judging myself irrevocably guilty. Maybe . . . I thought . . . maybe it was possible to have love without sex . . . or sex without love. Maybe that way it was possible to make a deal with the angels. Already, though, I was in an impossible bind, caught in the contemporary crossfire between mind, body, and feeling which had driven people far more mature than I into dark corners of desperation. Trying to distinguish nuances of truth, in order to find the one truth that would save me, I lost track of truth completely. There was, after all, nothing for me to go by, no way in which I could at least be true to my emotions by following them through to their natural conclusions, since I believed *beforehand* that those emotions had no right to exist, that they were stamped "invalid" by hidden powers.

It occurred to me somewhere along the line, however, that in order to come up with the right answers, I would have to play an endless game of blindman's bluff with my own psyche. For if I could no longer use the free flow of my feelings for a guideline, then I would never be sure whether or not the right answers were right for me.

This onslaught of confusion paralyzed my imagination, despite the fact that no one, as yet, had judged me at all. No one had said I was a leper. Yet I felt a leper, felt exiled from myself, felt that the gavel had struck twice and the judge had pronounced me guilty without explanation, sentencing me to limbo. I was wholly unable to proceed beyond my own sense of moral schizophrenia, my sense of being decent but damned. The moment I launched even a small-scale effort to come to terms with myself, conscience rushed in to ambush every impulse, until finally I found myself in a state of psychic anesthesia. What did I really feel? I didn't know. All I knew was that not feeling anything protected me from being tortured by the many-taloned demons of guilt and anxiety. And *that* was helpful.

There were times when I thought that something could be gained from talking seriously with someone, with anyone. But whom could I find? I might discuss the issue with some liberal-minded adult, except I had no way of finding out which adults were liberal-minded about such things without exposing my own fears. Small towns, moreover, are not noted for their liberal attitudes toward sexual deviations: the wilder members of our community would regard it as an interesting but morally neutral curiosity, and would have found my seriousness comical; the rest of the community would have shied away from the question altogether. Maybe there was *someone* in town who would have listened, but when I go through my mental list, I know that there was not one among them who could have tackled things head-on. Most probably they would have de-emphasized the issue so much that I would have been unable to reveal the depth of my own fear and confusion. Their own psychic imperatives would have forced them to cling to their ideas, while I, desperate to find the key to what they really felt, would sniff out every failure of conviction in their tone of voice, every wavering in their expression, every note of falsely hearty reassurance, until anything I might have had to say would be caught in the web of their own hidden uncertainties. If I were to insist on "confessing," it would seem that I had nothing to confess, and I, torn between my desire to be accepted and my desire to get it all out, would water down the force of things, trying to balance my words against their reactions, simply describing the events rather than the feelings connected to them. The events being ordinary enough, the case, almost certainly, would have been dismissed.

I might perhaps have turned to other kids at school, whose intellectual paraphernalia was less developed, and for whom the force of adolescent feeling would have had meaning. But kids didn't talk about things like that. They might discuss boy-girl sex with lurid graphicness, but anything else, if it existed in their lives at all, was confined to silent, inarticulate corners of the mind. Our experiences might have been similar, but we were all too isolated to know about it. The language of feeling being limited, passions were conveyed in phrases like, "He called me," "He's a dream," "I'm nuts about him." Further subtlety was beyond most of us.

There were, of course, books. The books I read, however, were whatever touched the raw nerves of sensibility, and I would have been hard put to find volumes in which lesbians were not judged for their perversion, not made to pay for their violation of social taboos. There was one: *The Second Sex.* The most eloquent testimony I have to the depth of my concern with the problem is that despite the difficulty of the book and my inability to comprehend huge chunks of it, the section on lesbianism has been so thoroughly thumbed in the copy I bought then and still have today that many of the pages have fallen out and whole paragraphs are underlined.

Outside of books, there were environments, like the theater, where lesbianism was certainly treated casually enough. I probably could have turned to those, except for the simple fact that *I* couldn't accept it casually and was vaguely suspicious of anyone who could. A puritan and a romantic, I was never quite at home with "wild living," although I was endlessly fascinated with it.

The truth of the matter was that by then I had already incorporated my parents' values and the values of their world. It was from *them* that I wanted—encouragement? understanding? serious thought? . . . something . . . anything that would make me feel I was human to the world I came from. My desire to be approved by all those people least likely to understand, let alone approve, any form of behavior other than their own, persisted undiminished for years, so that one side of me was fully capable of standing in judgment on precisely those actions that I didn't want to be judged for, while I continued to feel that the people who might really *accept* me were probably even more degenerate than I. If their standards led them to believe that lesbianism was as good a choice as anything else, then probably their standards just weren't high enough.

As for the man I fell in love with, his tolerance represented nothing more than his lack of sensitivity to the dimensions of the problem. It was many years before I came to understand that his concern, like many men's, was more a matter of ego than anything else, a notch-in-the-belt attitude of pseudo-chivalry which makes the woman "headed the wrong way" into a target for conversion. Nor did I know that men like him are easily stimulated by tales of two women and often fantasize themselves into a ménage where they are master of both. What I knew was that I had been told by a "sophisticated" person, a man to boot, that I was OK.

And so it was to him I turned for what little comfort could be gained during that time . . . for the sense that I was not completely penned in by what I might legitimately become, by a destiny that conceded nothing to individuality. It was all right, he said, for me to be a lesbian if that's what I was. But he said that while we were making love—when I believed most strongly that of course I wasn't a lesbian—I was really "his girl."

There were other times, though, when I continued to wonder, when my exhilarating and unprecedented sense of freedom transformed itself, so that I became uneasy, became conscious that somewhere along the line I had gone beyond my depth. Alone, away from the proof of my normality, I became obsessed with trying to figure out how much time there was before I had to be definitively cured. I knew that thoughts and feelings which were at least theoretically acceptable in adolescence, which were regarded as part of the rites of passage, would one day become symptoms of perversion. Lesbianism as part of a predetermined pattern of stages could be tolerated. But let it become less predictable or less easily confined, and it would become dangerous. No matter how much people might believe that sexual preferences were a matter of individual choice, they certainly would never want their daughters or their neighbors' daughters to turn out that way. How could I guarantee that another Rona wouldn't come along to disrupt my life?

It was fear of what might happen in the future rather than knowledge of what had already happened that dominated my thinking. I had no reason to believe that if I loved a woman once, I wouldn't love a woman again. Not having the benefit of clairvoyance, I lived in fear of that arbitrary moment when moral standards which had been temporarily suspended would once again be rigorously imposed.

Of course, anyone who is told that what is normal today will be taboo tomorrow will not have an easy time of things. The kind of existential flexibility that permits such a total living in the moment is rare in the extreme, and behavioral licenses that are revoked the instant one has the "wrong" birthday cannot help but create psyches capable of sustaining themselves only within the narrow corridors of compulsion.

I was scared. Period. There was just Jake to buttress me

against myself. And that wasn't going to last forever. Then what would happen? The question, whenever I allowed it to surface, made me queasy.

By the time I was eighteen I had left home, entered college, dropped out, and come back to live alone in New York. Whenever my eyes were drawn to an expressive female face on the street, whenever my interest in a woman started to rise beyond traditional thresholds, I would step back a little, push the off button and go on my way. I became less concerned with lesbianism and more concerned with being an independent woman. I took a job in film production, and in no time at all was so deeply immersed in glitter that I could scarcely open my eyes without a brilliant chip of it dropping in to obscure my vision. I was hardly ever out of love, and my loves included not only men, but the Plaza, Beekman Tower, Carl Schurz Park, the Staten Island ferry at dawn, and French crullers for breakfast. Champagne glasses tinkled in my blood. I wore high-heels and sexy clothes, and put on makeup so that no one could tell. I abandoned being a tomboy and became ultrafeminine, not so much because I thought I should be (although that surely was part of it), but because there was something newly sensual about being a woman, something languorous, provocative, and daring. I wanted to be exposed to everything, and made sure that I was; if someone made an interesting comment to me on the street, I went with them for coffee or cocktails; if someone invited me to their apartment, I accepted with blithe trust. I was convinced, in fact, that no matter what I did, some guardian angel who protected the innocent and even the half-innocent would steer my life on the right course. The skyscrapers of Manhattan were there to bend over me solicitously, to take care of my every need, to make sure that no one would hurt or disappoint me. I was a golden girl and New York was my crown.

Then I met Dee. Dee was working in the New School library, and I saw her there one day when I was reading up on the life of Eugene O'Neill. I stopped reading to watch her, mesmerized by her blatant yet at the same time reserved and enigmatic sexuality. By that time Rona already seemed very far away, and I felt as if my experience with her had been part of some other life. So I watched Dee, enjoying the effect she was having on otherwise determined students, and finally asked her to join me for coffee. She accepted, and we bought a box of cinnamon doughnuts at a grocery store on the corner, then sat in a late night coffee shop until closing time, leaning across the table toward each other with an eagerness and intensity that was unusual even for me. We had in common energy, enthusiasm, and a seemingly limitless receptivity to experience. Dee, coming to New York fresh from the Midwest, had to keep moving twenty-four hours a day in order to catch up with as much of the city as possible. She seemed to be running on an adrenaline overflow, and had to talk fast because she had an infinite number of things to say. So did I. Both of us had lives that were equally rich and chaotic, although entirely different. What Dee wanted from the city was the chance to meet people who saw life from new perspectives, people who wouldn't be overwhelmed by the barrage of questions that accumulated in her head during the two or three hours a night when she sometimes managed to sleep. She wanted knowledge, and wanted to meet everyone who might possess a corner of it. Having grown up in a wealthy semi-socialite environment, she found glamour boring. I, on the other hand, was infatuated with glamour, and wanted to discover every inch of territory in the city that I hadn't been exposed to growing up as a neighborhood kid in New York. I wanted to know the East Side, upper and lower, and to know eight million people intimately. I wanted to make the city streets my kingdom. So I walked those streets every night, sometimes until three in the morning, trying to drain off some of the energy that accumulated inside of me so fast I could barely keep up with it. Given our hyperactive constitutions, neither Dee nor I had any time for amenities, and by the time the coffee shop closed, we had exchanged so many details about our lives and thoughts and feelings that afterward I couldn't remember a word of what we'd said.

By then I was already in a trance, firmly and unambiguously in love with her. I had no thoughts at all about Rona. Instead, I had endless fantasies about what it would be like to have a real friend. Years of being without one, and then, all of a sudden, there she was. It was the kind of friendship that forms only during that particular period of one's life . . . when one has energy and love enough to dispense in giant cranefuls, when one's basic philosophy is to trust people until they have proved finally and irrevocably that they cannot be trusted, when openness and enthusiasm are at their peak. The friendships that manage to survive such times seem to bridge a span of life that looms so large in one's past that they become almost unassailable.

Neither Dee nor I was naive. We both had had experience with betrayal and hurt, but not enough experience to make us believe that it was the rule rather than the exception. Because of that, we were able to hand our spirits over to one another with a confidence that was almost sacramental.

Soon after we met, we decided to sublet an apartment together. The apartment belonged to a contemporary musician and his wife, and there were books and sheet music piled up to the ceiling, a grand piano in the living room, and a double bed in the bedroom. I ransacked the library in search of poems, plays, and novels, and discovered that many of the contemporary works had authorial inscriptions on the flyleafs. Dee ransacked the neighborhood and brought home everyone she could find who possessed even a grain of originality. There was a constant flow of people in and out of the house, and someone was always playing sonatas on the piano or singing arias. Both of us stayed up almost all night every night, talking, and then slept nude in the same bed with our arms wrapped around each other. Some nights I would vacate the bed for a male friend of hers, and twice she did the same for me. I envied her charisma, her beauty, her brilliance, and her audacity. When we curled up in bed together, there was an ache of excess warmth and energy in both of us, which made us hold each other very close, even though I, at least, was never aware of a real desire to make love. There was a chemistry and magnetism between us, though, that seemed to have no name and no shape. It clung to us whenever we walked down the street together, so that people were always staring at us as we strode shoulder to shoulder or sometimes even hip to hip. I was never sure whether the stares were because Dee was so strikingly beautiful, or because some invisible aura of "that perversion" hung over us. I was defiant about that perversion by then and said scornfully that even New Yorkers were provincial. I loved Dee so much it didn't matter to me what *anyone* said. In fact, I think I even *wanted* people to think the worst, wanted them to think we were free enough to express our closeness in every way possible.

The truth was, though, that I would never have dared to do anything more than hold Dee, and no matter how deep my love for her was, I still considered her just a friend. As in the eighth grade, friendship was still secondary to loving a man. It didn't matter to me that every time one of my relationships broke up, it was Dee I came to for comfort, Dee I dared cry in front of, Dee who would make phone calls to my office saying I was sick and couldn't come to work, Dee who understood every nuance of desire, compulsion, romantic fatalism, and melodramatic pretension that crisscrossed my life. It didn't matter that, even after we moved into separate apartments, our friendship endured longer than any other love relationship did. It didn't matter that every time I looked at her, with her natural, slightly lavender eyelids, her hair like Botticelli's Venus, and the form of her body so strikingly similar to Steiglitz's photographs of Georgia O'Keefe, my blood felt like marmalade. No matter that for eight years, whenever we talked, the history of our intimacy resonated behind our growing disagreements over politics, art, drugs, and the way to live our lives. No matter what happened or what I felt, Dee remained just a friend.

For nearly eight years we virtually ignored the question of sexuality, even though the sense of it pervaded our every contact with one another. But then suddenly, something changed. Whenever Dee and I got together, Dee would bring up the subject of lesbianism, talking about how women who loved each other ought to be free to express that love in every way. I said of course, but added that I didn't think it was exactly normal. Dee said, "Well, what's normal?" Bit by bit I felt the ground slipping out from under me, and in a burst of excess panic, I challenged her on every point. Then she lapsed into silence, becoming hidden and vulnerable, unable to argue about something so close to the heart of our own lives.

I began to feel terrible, began to feel estranged and frustrated and confused and unhappy. Disaster after disaster had brought my sexual life with men to a grinding halt, and I wanted nothing more than to renew it, to find some decent, wholesome way of living. I wanted to be happy, wanted to fall in love again, wanted to lead a simple, normal life. Often the thought crossed my mind that maybe, throughout all those years of falling in and out of love with men, I had been a repressed lesbian. If that was so, then I didn't even want to know about it. So long as I had been basking in the sunlight of sexual confidence, so long as I'd been in love with a man, I could be triumphantly exhibitionist about my intimacy with Dee, could say and mean that I didn't care what people thought. Now, though, when everything was uncertain, when my whole life was in a state of upheaval, the last thing I wanted was to add another conflict to it.

So everything Dee said about lesbianism I denied, acutely aware that if she were to have an intimate sexual relationship with a woman, I would be the most likely woman for her to have it with.

For almost a year, I could feel the tension from those conversations resonating throughout every meeting we had. I was afraid to touch her now, afraid of what might happen. There was a wedge in our friendship which had never been there before. True, our lives had gone in completely different directions, hers toward radical politics and mine toward art. True, she believed in collective living and collective thinking, while I was a *petit-bourgeois* individualist to the core. True, she was optimistic about the future of humanity, whereas I was increasingly cynical. True, she was still willing to try just about anything, while I, after almost ten years of treating my life as an experiment, wanted nothing more than peace, quiet, and the most conventional kind of love.

Those things had never inhibited our friendship before. But now, with the "new thing," they did. Dee's interpretations of the meaning of lesbianism became more and more theoretical, more and more abstract. She said that someday we would all be practicing bisexuals. I began to feel stifled, and one day in the midst of a heated discussion

I burst out with, "Dee, I'm sick of discussing it. If you think it's so important, why don't we just *do* it." I was shocked at my own bravado. But I knew that I couldn't retreat, that I had called her a coward for just talking about it, even though I knew I was equally a coward. We looked at each other awkwardly, embarrassedly. Then, as if we were going to an execution, we walked into the bedroom and lay down on the bed next to each other.

All of the things that had always been natural between us were now suddenly charged with meaning, charged with sexuality. I, who was so used to holding her in my arms, suddenly didn't know how to do it. We lay there, strapped in our own sense of obligation, hoping for the upsurge of a passion which might make the experience real. I was watching myself, being the observer, hoping that with this one try I would find out what my true impulses were. But I didn't seem to *have* any impulses. Under the pressures of an irrevocable decision, we moved our hands over each other's bodies, carefully avoiding the "erogenous zones," feeling a shyness and timidity which inhibited both of us. It was strange to be touching another woman, strange and somehow mechanical, even though my heart was pounding, and I could feel that old, familiar throbbing inside of me. It was just like with a man, I thought. And knew that wasn't true. I was too conscious of the familiarity of angles, curves, and hollows so much like my own, for it to be true. I felt as if I was making love to myself, felt intimate and estranged all at once.

Then the phone rang. It was a man I'd been attracted to for a long time, but had never been intimate with. I could hear my own voice on the telephone, with all of the pent-up sexuality transferred whole from the lovemaking with Dee to the attachment I felt to him. I was overwhelmed by my sense of immediacy and desperately afraid that he would notice my tremors of shyness, intensity, and passion.

After I hung up, I went back to lie down next to Dee again, feeling that this time I *had* to go through with it. But she said, "You know we don't have to rush things. Neither of us are hung up on the act." I felt a great surge of relief, along with an equivalent stab of unhappiness, which I would have preferred to ignore.

Within moments, though, the unhappiness had forced itself to the forefront of my imagination, and I found myself thinking: Would a man have done that? Would a man say we don't have to rush things? Of course I knew that we had stopped as much out of fear and inhibition as from concern for each other's vulnerability. Still . . . it would be totally unlike Dee to be sexually demanding, to insist that sex should have a final aim. For years, she, like myself, had been satisfied with simple warmth, tenderness, and affection. There might be a *desire* to do more, but desire could always wait. That was a real difference between most women and most men, or at least the men and women I knew. For men, sex was aim oriented. There was a beginning, a middle, and an end. For me, and for many other women, it had never been that way. Kissing Dee was just as important as sharing an orgasm. It was that way for her as well as for me. The real pleasure came from intimacy in all of its forms. Dee could afford to say, "We don't have to rush things." So could I. There was none of the frantic concern with "Doing it" that was such a crucial part of relations with men. There was just being close. Whatever happened would happen.

I suddenly remembered a line from *The Bell Jar:* "What does a woman see in a woman that she can't see in a man?" And the answer: "Tenderness"—which had stayed with me long after the rest of the book faded. Often, I found myself thinking, "It's true, it's true," found myself wishing at the same time that it wasn't, trying to think of men who were genuinely tender. Certainly there were a few, but more often than not the tenderness was accompanied by a kind of softness that indicated a lack of shape, and seemed to exist by default. Rarely was it a delicate vein in a strong constitution. *That* was what I wanted: the tenderness that was a counterpoint to virility.

Among women, however, tenderness could almost be assumed. It was strength that had to be sought for in the creation of a true balance.

The problem of combining strength and tenderness had less to do with sexual performance than with total personality. Men, it seemed, were always surprised when a woman cared less about their performance than she did about the quality of their feelings. They were far more frightened of being judged for their sexual inadequacy than for their inadequacy as people. Since most men only reluctantly put up with a woman's sexual hesitations or incapacities, they take it for granted that a woman will only reluctantly put up with theirs. They assume that what a woman really requires is the perfect orgasm. It is

an assumption based more upon their own require
than upon a knowledge of women, for whom sex is a s
of being as well as an action.

Women—at least the women I know—are by and large tolerant of sexual frailty, more inclined to feel concern for a man who is "inadequate" than to feel scorn, more inclined to feel voided when tenderness that *cannot* be faked is absent. (Perhaps since the women I know tend to be rather strong individuals, they can afford the luxury of giving leeway to the variations in human capacities at any given moment.) They know that inadequacy, in itself, can even sometimes become a vehicle for transmitting tenderness in a world where tenderness must find reasons to justify itself, whereas sex is considered self-justifying.

Of course, under ideal conditions, I too would want a wholly adequate lover—"adequate" meaning sensitive, enthusiastic, imaginative, spontaneous, and affectionate as well as potent; I would hope to be adequate in all of the same ways. In less than ideal conditions, however, I would prefer to be in bed with a man whose overenthusiastic fantasies, pent-up sexual drive, and authentic involvement make him ejaculate prematurely, than to have sex with a man who can keep it up for an hour because he does daily exercises, testing himself out on every woman he can find. A little awkwardness can be far more personal than a lot of polish. Spectacular showmanship, while it can leave you breathless with excitement, seems like a sadly empty performance arena once the tents have folded. As for "skills," no woman wants a technocrat in bed next to her; she wants a human being like herself. Women, far

em to sense that it is possible to be
r and human at the same time. They
on't always require immediate satis-
he long run everyone wants to get
le satisfaction, physical and other-
y know that the coldness of a man who rolls over and away when "it" is done, is at least as important, if not more important, than the heat he generates in the thick of things.

Women know . . . the thought made me want to cry. I wanted men to know, wanted them to know not from what I or anyone else might tell them, but from the evidence of their own senses, their own feelings.

The words, "We don't have to rush things," are not part of a tactic of seduction; they are part of an awareness of the subtle shadings of human feeling. I wanted for men to be able to say that too, and felt that as long as they couldn't or wouldn't, lesbian relationships really might constitute a threat to traditional male-female relationships *even* among women who have no particularly strong erotic drives toward other women. Women were frustrated, that was certain. I too was frustrated, frustrated most severely by the misplaced emphasis on cheap sex and the lack of emphasis on real feeling. Tenderness is a basic requirement of life. So is understanding, or affection. So is sex. But unless they all can be brought together, I suspect that women are going to start turning in increasing numbers to their own kind for comfort as well as sustenance.

Why should that be surprising, though? Don't men value what they call the "personal touch," the felt knowledge, the sympathy, the tenderness, which, according to their own standards of femininity, only a woman can offer? Shouldn't it be natural that women, if they value themselves at all, would *also* value those characteristics, also have those needs, would seek to satisfy them in their relationships with men, and when they failed, would turn, just as men do, to other women for their fulfillment?

Dee and I lay on the bed for a long time. I held her in my arms and smelled the slightly sour scent of her hair. We didn't talk at all. Over and over again, the aching unhappiness that had come over me when Dee said, "We don't have to rush," the unhappiness of knowing what a rare and unaccustomed thing that was, returned, larger each time.

After a while I got up from the bed, walked into the bathroom, looked into the mirror and brought my face up close to it. Then I laid my cheek against the coolness of the glass and burst into tears. When I stopped crying, the mirror was so fogged that I couldn't even see my reflection any more.

Over the next year Dee and I saw very little of each other. I had been more frightened by our experiment than I cared to admit, and my fear had made me feel an irrational fury toward her for making me face things I would rather have ignored—despite the fact that it was I who had challenged her that afternoon to put up or shut up.

ry time we got together, there was a tension and discomfort in our conversations, a hesitation in our expressions, and, above all, an unwillingness to demonstrate the affection that always before we had shown so openly.

It was almost a year later, on a snowy New Year's night, that Dee and I stood together in Central Park, as estranged from one another as we had ever been in the entire history of our friendship. Dee said that she had been thinking about joining Gay Liberation. She said that she identified with other women and wanted to be free to love them. I listened, and then screamed at her, screamed through the cold and the brightness and the fierceness of the night snowflakes, screamed, "Dee, you're *not* a lesbian. You're not—I know you!" Then I cried and she cried. She said I wasn't giving her a chance to be herself. She said I was just scared. I refused to listen. We walked out of the park together. And it seemed that once again, as in that faraway time with Lisa, the very backbone of a friendship had been broken.

All of those experiences taught me something, though, taught me how easy it is to be tolerant for other people, how difficult when one is forced finally to face and be tolerant of oneself. Like the liberals of the sixties who had "nothing against intermarriage" but balked when their sons and daughters brought home the black men and women they intended to marry, or like the Jews who were all for civil rights until it was their own jobs that were threatened by the inroads that blacks were making into the professions, I too discovered that saying "people's sexual preferences are their business" was very different from saying that my sexual preferences were no one's business. I knew that society, or at least the kind of society I lived in, didn't make a grand fuss about lesbianism any more. But I also knew that when it came to confronting that society, or even confronting myself with the possibility of being a lesbian, the gap between my beliefs and my fears was almost insurmountable.

I realized once again how painful the struggle could be when I saw another person going through it. I was at a Boston Women's Liberation meeting with Dee during that period of time when we were still trying to patch up our friendship. In the middle of the meeting, a woman stood up and said that, to her, talking about women's relations with men just wasn't worth it. "We're lesbians," she said, gesturing in the direction of several women who were grouped around her. "We love other women. And we want to know how you feel about *that,* whether you're willing to accept *us* as sisters too."

Suddenly everyone in the room became attentive. Several women swiveled around in their chairs to stare, realized that they were being conspicuously curious, and swiveled back again. After a slow, thirty-second pause, a vehement chorus of, "We don't care," "The movement includes all women," and "So what" began to echo throughout the room. The chorus, however, was not terribly convincing, since it was too loud and too emphatic to be believable, and since the stares had all but canceled out the pretense of casualness. I found myself concentrating on the use of the word "sisters," thinking that I hated the word, and didn't consider *anyone* my sister, least of all complete strangers, until I suddenly realized that my preoccupation with the use of an irritating word had deflected me completely from the real issue. I was seized with a sense of guilt. What in God's name was I afraid of? I thought. Why couldn't I bear to face the question?

"I don't want to know what you think," one of the women said. "I want to know what you feel."

"I feel fine. What difference does it make?" a woman answered defensively.

"Yeah," said another. "It doesn't make any difference."

The woman who had called herself a lesbian stopped for a moment and looked around the room. "I don't believe you," she said. "You're just being good liberals, no different from a lot of men who say they believe in women's lib. Being a lesbian *is* different, whether you say so or not. It's different because the world says so, and because when I lost my job as a teacher last year, it didn't have anything to do with what kind of teacher or what kind of person I was. It was because the one thing that *counted* to that school was the fact that I was a lesbian, that I loved other women. A fact that really has no more to do with who I am than the fact that I'm shy or read a lot of books or like teaching school. My sexual identity was what defined me to those people, and it's what defines me to you, too. So don't kid yourself. Go to a party some time and listen to the conversation around you. Mrs. So-and-So points to someone across the room and says that she's the editor of a magazine . . . he's a film director . . . he's set up an experimental school . . . she's an analyst . . . she's a member of a law commune . . . and she, you see that one over there, she's a lesbian."

She didn't need to go on. Her party story was exaggerated, and she was probably somewhat paranoid, but still what she was describing was in some important sense true. The hostess might be *proud* of having acquired a lesbian to come to her party, and not condescending, but chances were that, in either case, the woman's being a lesbian was high on her list of vital pieces of information. And if the young woman was paranoid there was nothing so strange about that. After all, hadn't I, too, been paranoid? Wasn't paranoia an almost inevitable consequence of the kinds of experiences lesbians (and, in some respects, all women) have to go through on a daily basis?

What the problem came down to was that there didn't seem to be any way of looking at lesbians as individuals, since in "the most important thing" they were all the same. It was impossible to imagine a party hostess pointing to someone across the room and saying, "You see that one over there, she's a heterosexual." It would seem perfectly ludicrous. And besides, who would *care?* But if you're a lesbian, almost everyone cares, whether overtly or covertly. Everyone is either fascinated or repelled, but seldom is anyone indifferent. Even for us at that meeting, women who presumably regarded all other women as "sisters," the word "lesbian" had the sound of witchcraft in it, the sound of detonating explosives.

I looked at the woman who had just spoken. She was attractive, and I was relieved. But then I became angry at myself for caring. "Look," I said to myself. "A lesbian is a person. She's no more nor less of a person because she's attractive." But for me, whether I liked to admit it or not, attractiveness made a difference. A lesbian woman who was attractive could never be suspected of a sour grapes attitude, of "settling" for her own kind because men weren't interested in her. And not only that, but *I* was drawn to women whom I considered attractive. Attractiveness meant a great many things. It had nothing to do with being "pretty," but had a lot to do with vividness, with a certain personal stamp that made someone stand out in a group, with a rare blend of awkwardness and grace, shyness and confidence, warmth and restraint, sexuality and coolness. There were people I found attractive and others I didn't. Nothing could be done about it.

Nor could anything be done about the fact that I often found lesbians attractive precisely *because* they were lesbians. Actually, when it came right down to it, I was attracted to or interested in *everyone* because of something unique in that person, in some element that made that person's life separate, and by that separateness, more whole. But was being interested in a woman because she was a lesbian any worse than being interested in an architect because of his buildings, or a teacher because of her ideas? Lesbians were marked, many of them in the best sense of the word; marked by struggle . . . they do what they have to do . . . they are what they must be.

Suddenly, though, all of the thoughts about what lesbians were stopped, and I was left with just one. "And you yourself? What are you?"

"All right," the self-declared lesbian said. "Let's say it's OK with you that I'm a lesbian, that it's OK for me to love my sisters. Let's assume you really mean that. But how would you feel if one day you realized that your sister or your best friend or maybe even *you* were a lesbian?"

She had touched home base. There was a sound in the room that was not quite a sound, but more like a presence making itself known. It was the sound of bones stiffening, eyelids shutting, breaths catching, hands locking. It was the sound of reflexes that for a moment were more powerful than any impulse for tolerance, discretion, or understanding.

A screw tightened inside of me. I was hanging on the other women's reactions as much as the lesbian was. Lisa and Rona and Dee were all hanging on the reactions, their faces fresh in my imagination again, anxious faces, waiting faces, uncertain and vulnerable faces. Among their faces was my own, just as anxious, just as vulnerable.

The young woman smiled, a little bit bitterly, into the growing silence. I sat there, thinking that I ought to say something but not knowing what. Then suddenly I knew. What she wanted was what I wanted: just an open admission of how frightened we all were without our armor of "decency" to protect us. Hadn't I so often said that I couldn't tolerate the depersonalized understanding that men offered to women in the name of peace and harmony? Wasn't I now on the other side of the fence (or at least straddling it), forced to confront my own lack of understanding . . . more than anything, about my own self? Of course, if I separated that self from the problem, if I considered it "objectively" and granted my understanding to others on an impersonal basis, on a basis that finally would cost me absolutely nothing, trying only to salvage my personal invulnerability, then I would be trapped in my own psychic spider web.

If I did that, there would be no place for the lesbians to go, except to another room, to another meeting among their own kind, where being tolerated was not a game to be played out among expansive "sisters," where tolerance was not a problem at all, and there were other problems to work out. Perhaps when it came right down to it, there would be no place for me to go either.

I spoke finally and could hear the vibrato in my voice, even though the words came out evenly spaced and controlled.

"I accept it, I think. But it also scares me. It scares me most of all about myself. Because I don't know. I really don't know. I've never been able to find out. And the thought that I might be . . ." I couldn't finish the sentence. There was no way to. Everything was unresolved.

The woman looked at me and smiled. "Congratulations," she said. "It's about time."

I hadn't the courage to smile back at her. Already I was soaked in sweat. And I was aware of Dee, sitting there, far away on the other side of the room.

Annie was asleep on the living room couch, exhausted after traveling ten hours from the city to my house in

Maine. I had only met her once before, but had learned from that first conversation in the middle of a roomful of people that she was a radical therapist and bisexual. Also that she was struggling to get over a love affair with a woman. Now, desperate to escape from the city, to think, to order her feelings, to break the depression that had been with her ever since she and Barbara decided to separate, she had come to my house, planning to stay at least a week.

I looked at the books she had with her: *The Dialectic of Sex: A Case For Feminist Revolution, Women and Their Bodies, Sexual Politics.* I could hear the echoes of oppression reverberating through her dreams, could see lines of feminist women marching across my lawn with their arms linked, waving banners that said, GAY IS PROUD. All the women were smiling.

In my dream of a few nights before, the women were walking across the water wearing long dresses and Garbo hats. Also smiling. Except they were debutantes. And waved no banners. I was condescending toward them for being banal and superficial.

To me now they all seemed the same . . . legions of women all the same. I was in revolt against legions, all kinds of legions. It had been over a year since that meeting in Boston, and in that time I had decided (as if such things could ever be decided) that I wasn't really a lesbian. Hostile toward men, yes. Scared of them, yes. But a lesbian, no. For now, I wanted no more grand passions of any kind. No more movements or schemes or legions or tracts.

No more absolute virtue for men or women. No more gaping holes to come like craters of the moon between me and ordinariness. Like cotton candy, double-decker busses, Hollywood movies . . . the nostalgia for a way of life that never was, a bright, mirrored sliver of no-time lodged between cymbals crashing, the split image of the age (my age), the schizophrenic longing for all the commitments and none of them, the desire to be . . . whatever, just be . . . the desire for (I didn't care if it wasn't what they'd cracked it up to be) simple, water-logged, brain-damaged happiness . . . the sheer banality of that rare and elusive bird called "a regular family life." That was what I wanted.

In pursuit of precisely such happiness, I had invited a friend of mine and his two children to stay at my house during their summer vacation. For weeks I had been caught up in playing at domesticity; already I had forgotten where the game ended and the reality took over. The children stared, fascinated, at Annie's red Afro fanning out around her head and I thought that I would never succeed in making the transition from domestic tranquillity to revolutionary fervor, but then we all started to pack up the car and I forgot about transitions. Within an hour sea anemones, mussel shells, lobster buoys, bathing suits, sleeping bags, and an inflatable raft were loaded up and the family was ready to leave.

I kissed Mark goodbye. It was the first time in a long time that I had completely meant a kiss. Three years of rabid mistrust, of nearly complete abstinence, of tapeworms chewing up my insides. And now, finally, I felt close to a man. Even as I kissed him I was aware of Annie watching us. "Too late Orphan Annie, you're just too late," I thought. And hoped that it was true.

Annie was sitting in the rocking chair. All eyes and flaming halo. And a look of small concentrated aloneness. There was a silence between us, a silence traversed by the steps of phantom thoughts.

"It made me feel like crying," she said finally.

"What did?"

"The way the children kissed the trees."

"Oh." It had made me feel like crying too. Both children going from tree to tree and kissing the trunks. Every tree. There was something about the passion and possessiveness of the gesture that made the land theirs more completely than it had ever been mine.

"You all seemed to be very close," Annie said.

"In some ways we are."

"Well," Annie said, stretching in the chair. "That's cool." Then she laughed, and I thought, now why couldn't she have said something like "Families are obsolete," or "How unliberated." If she had done that, things would have been easier. I could have dismissed her, forgotten her, ground her up in my mental dispose-all and flushed her down the drain.

But Annie refused to be flushed. She insisted on being a person.

"I'm not gay you know," I said.

She looked at me strangely for a moment and then said, "Are you supposed to be?"

After that we lit a joint, and sat there in the living room of my house in Maine, smoking together.

"Are you attracted to me?" I asked her when the dope had begun to spiral through my head.

"I could be," she said. "But you said you're not gay and I don't like to force myself on people. Besides, I'm still in love with Barbara."

"Oh, I guess I thought that if you were a lesbian, you were attracted to all women."

"I'm not. Right now I'm just attracted to one . . . Barbara."

"Oh."

"We were friends for six years before it turned into an affair. It was my first affair with a woman, and I fell in love with her."

I could feel the spaces changing already, feel all the newly acquired proportions stretching out of shape. Annie was not going to talk about "lesbian relationships." She wasn't even going to allow me to think of lesbianism. She was just going to say . . . I fell in love with her, the way I would say it about a man, the way I once said it about Dee . . .

"The biggest problem was that Barbara was married. She still is. She couldn't talk about it with her husband. He wouldn't have believed her anyway. It was too threatening to him. She kept thinking that she was a terrible person, and I felt responsible. Barbara's very straightforward and she couldn't stand the deceptions. She said the whole thing was going to make her crack, it was going to drive her crazy. We were always having to meet secretly. I couldn't call her at home. When I needed her, she was with her husband. I'd meet her at her shrink's office, and once, when she came out, she wasn't able to look at me. She told me she'd decided to have a baby. She said she'd told her shrink there was nothing a man could do for her any more, except that. Having a baby was her way of ending things between us, though. I said, 'Barbara, we could bring up the baby ourselves.' When I said that she started to cry. Then she laughed. The strain was too much for her. Finally we decided to stop seeing each other. Now I'm trying to get myself back together."

I wanted to put my arms around her. There was something strong but at the same time fragile about her, something uncompromisingly direct and fiercely proud. But I hardly knew her. And even though she'd said that she wasn't turned on to all women, the residues of my experience with men were still with me: I expected that touching someone who *might* respond to me sexually was a dangerous thing, that it had to lead to making love, had to be interpreted as a provocation. I didn't yet realize that one of the special things about many "new lesbians" was precisely their respect for the dimensions of things, their willingness to let a gesture be a gesture, their ability to distinguish between expressions of warmth and expressions of passion, and to value each, both separately and in unison. All I thought was that Annie was a lesbian.

So I decided not to put my arms around her. Instead, I thought about what it was like to be involved with someone who was married, just someone, not a man or a woman particularly. A person you have to share with another person.

"It's strange," I said. "When you talk about your affair with Barbara, it sounds in a lot of ways like my affairs with married men."

"In some ways, maybe," she said. "In other ways not. But I guess that gives us something in common, even though you're not gay."

I looked at her through the smoke and thought that maybe I would tell her about Rona and Lisa and Dee.

"I guess it does," I said. And smiled at her.

"I was in therapy for five years," Annie said. "And for two and a half of them I didn't talk at all. I was always outgoing, but I'd never in my life talked about anything personal. So I sat there, for that whole time, and said nothing. When I quit last month, the last thing I said to my shrink was, 'Well, which do you think it will be—a man or a woman?' He laughed and said he didn't think I'd given up on men yet. He would have preferred for it to be a man, of course. He was a Freudian, but even so, he never pushed me to change. He'd talk about my relationships with men and my relationships with women as if they were all the same. He didn't make any distinctions. That was one of the best things about him. For a long time though, I thought being gay was terrible.

"I had a patient, a girl I identified with. She was gay and I was having a terrible time with her, because basically I thought it was wrong. I wanted her to change. But I wasn't getting anywhere, so one day I talked with my supervisor. I told him she was homosexual. He asked me what I thought about it. I said I thought it was bad for her because society was against it. He said I was crazy. Then he asked me what I thought about it for myself. And I told him the same thing. I said I would feel guilty. He said what the hell did I have to feel guilty for. I didn't have an answer. We talked for about two hours. Finally he said, 'Listen, you never cared what society thought about *anything.* You've always done exactly what you wanted to do. And now you're saying you wouldn't do something because society condemns it, because society says it's bad. Just *think* about that.' I thought about it, and after I finished thinking, I stopped feeling guilty. A few months later the last barrier went and I got sexually involved with Barbara. That was a year and a half ago. And now . . . well, now I tell everyone when they get depressed that before they kill themselves they should first have an affair with a woman."

I cooked dinner, and poured out two glasses of wine. Annie had been lying on the couch in the living room thinking stoned thoughts. Now she came into the kitchen. Her face was very sober.

"You know," she said, "I just had an incredible insight. I love to be fed. And Barbara loved to feed me. I thought of myself as the provider. I could provide for both of us. It was funny because my father never did that. And whenever I was with a man, I thought I wouldn't be given enough to eat. That he would take most of it. When I was a kid I always had horrible food. And whatever there was, my father would get the best. So now with a woman, I think, well, I can take care of both of us. I'll be fed, and I can make sure she'll get fed."

I filled her plate with fish and broccoli. "Didn't you ever think that maybe you could have a relationship with a man where you would take care of each other? If he couldn't provide for you, you would provide for him? Or both of you would work?"

"Uh uh. I never felt I had the same rights with a man. Or the same control. With a woman there weren't any categories about who was supposed to provide for whom. I knew I could count on myself. With a man, there was too much old baggage to start shifting around."

"But Annie," I said, "you're not really changing anything in your relationship with a woman. You're just taking on the old role that men used to have. You're protecting yourself by being the one in control."

"But with a woman it works out differently. There's no power in it any more. We're just taking care of each other in the ways we know how."

Annie had a second helping of fish and broccoli. Together we finished off the wine.

. . .

I finally told her about Rona and Dee, leaving out the story of Lisa. Somehow, even though it was the farthest away, it was still the most dangerous. Perhaps because it was so specifically sexual. And because if I thought about what we'd done, I would have to think about what women do.

So instead of mentioning Lisa, I said, "You know, every time I've tried to think what it would be like to have sex with another woman, I get as far as touching her breast. And then I can't imagine what I'd do next. It all seems so strange."

"That's the way it was with Barbara and me the first time," Annie said. "We didn't know either. All I could imagine was women holding each other."

I thought of Dee again, of the times she'd held me, of that afternoon on the bed. Again the ache that I'd thought was gone came back over me. By this time Annie and I were sitting on the floor. The wine had loosened both of us, and we had smoked another joint. I was beginning to feel that maybe it would be possible to talk to her without pretension or falsity. What was both disconcerting and attractive about Annie was that she made the moral criteria that I had clung to so tenaciously seem extraneous, even though she was a moral person . . . moral in the sense of being true to herself, of struggling for authenticity and commitment. Not only that, but she had passions, and they were fine-grained. She was honest enough that there seemed to be only one way to respond to her—with an equivalent honesty.

So I took the plunge. "Look," I said, "you know what I said about not being gay. I don't know if it's true."

"Oh," she said. "Revelation."

She passed me the newly opened bottle of wine, and I drank.

"I've never really been sure about myself," I said, stretching out full length on the floor. "All sorts of things happen in my dreams. But I only have the dreams when things go wrong with men. I've never been able to figure out whether things go wrong with them because I don't want them to go right, because deep down I'm a lesbian, or whether I think I'm a lesbian because things go wrong with men . . . as a defense against loving them. But, somehow, even though there's so much that *doesn't* happen with men, so much that they don't do, I still keep trying, keep hoping that . . . I don't know. Maybe it's nothing but masochism."

"It is," Annie said. "I used to be exactly like that, always thinking: Well, I'll work it out with a man. But all of the things I was struggling to get out of my relationships with men, I got right away from the relationships with women. For instance, with a woman, we could go on making love for days. Everything was sensual. There was always affection. Things were connected. It wasn't a matter of click on, click off . . . do this, do that."

A picture of Mark flashed through my mind, Mark in the morning, scarcely seeming to know me, Mark at night, intensely physical, intensely passionate. "Why?" I had said to him. "Why should the morning be any different? All I want is five minutes of your time, five minutes so I don't have to feel I've been sleeping with a stranger."

And he had said, "I'll try."

But the effort had been false. It just hadn't come naturally to him. Maybe it never would. Were all men like that? Why did it come naturally to me? What was wrong with them?

The tension was starting to build up in me again. Annie was saying all of the things I'd been feeling, except she was *acting* on those feelings, whereas I was trying to dispose of them.

Why did one person act on them, and another person try to dispose of them? There had to be other things involved besides dissatisfactions and frustrations, things that were even stronger than the power of repression. Not just preferences, but drives. Not just disappointments, but desires.

"I keep thinking that men can learn," I said. "They have to learn."

"They have to but they don't. A woman I know was living with a man for fourteen months. She kept trying. But nothing happened. After a while she started to wonder why she was trying so hard, making impossible demands, when with a woman the demands weren't even necessary. That's a real question."

"I suppose that if you have strong enough feelings for a man in the first place, you want to keep on working at it with him. It's true that it's easier to be close to a woman: there's more affection, more give, less fighting just to be yourself. But I still seem to need men. No matter how much I thrash around, I always end up with that. The need isn't just sexual, but sex has something to do with it. What men don't realize . . . half the time they don't care . . . is that all of those other things like concern and affection and understanding go into sex too. Once they know the basic need is there, their egos are satisfied. They think: Well, if she's turned on to me I don't have to bother with the rest. And that makes me fight against even admitting that I need them at all."

"Do you want to spend your whole life teaching men how to be human?" Annie asked.

"No."

"Do you want some happiness for yourself?"

"Yes."

"Well?"

I didn't know what to say.

It was a few days later that we started talking about sex. At first we were both very tentative. The sense of privacy that had been ingrained in us throughout our lives was still there, a kind of puritan reserve that made us balk at talking openly about intimacy. Gradually, though, we got down to the simple questions of anatomy . . . and the part it plays in destiny. For me, there was ultimately the sense that even though whole bodies were involved in sex, even though there were definite pleasures involved in unconsummated sex, pleasures great enough that I always enjoyed touching and being touched—still, one of the greatest pleasures was having a man inside of me. I could stay that way for hours, fall asleep that way, have orgasms or not have orgasms. But that in itself was a whole experience . . . an important one. There was a sense of fullness attached to it, a sense of completion.

For Annie, the opposite was true. Penises were usually an unwelcome intrusion. "Every time a man was inside of me," she said, "I felt I was being used, that I was there for his pleasure. No matter who was on top, it was always me who was being pinned down. With a woman things are more subtle, more spread out. You never feel ripped up inside. The only men I've ever been able to enjoy sex with were men I didn't give a shit about. Then I could let go, because I didn't feel vulnerable. And not being vulnerable, I was like them. As soon as I started to care about someone, I would tighten up. I was just too scared of letting them reach me and use their power. With men it always has to do with power."

It was strange. I agreed with her. And had felt all of those things. But I had felt them *alongside* of the pleasure. Fear, hostility, anger, the sense of being violated . . . all of that was there. But so was the sense of being organically whole, of reaching some ultimate kind of fusion. It was only in love (and even there it was rare enough) that the sense of fulfillment completely outstripped the sense of anger. When love and sex were right with a man, the world seemed solid, real, dependable, even if only momentarily. When sex and love were wrong, I felt as if my life was being flushed along like raw sewage. But in order for sex to be right, so many things had to happen, so many emotions had to be shaped and molded and welded together. What did the sheer persistence in doing that come from? Even though loving a man and having sex with him often seemed more like living in a bomb shelter than under a security blanket, I still kept trying, while there rarely seemed to be enough of a drive in me to act on my attractions for women, despite my awareness that in many ways it might be much more satisfying.

Was that only because of sex? Because of love? Was even love—finally—enough? Or was that too a pipe dream belonging to some ancient cartographer's chart of the universe? What if everything went sour with a man? How long could you hold on to that faith, the deeply rooted belief that, ultimately, you belonged together with men?

Something in me needed to retain the faith. Whether that was due to courage and persistence, or fear and repression, I couldn't say for sure. All I could say was that I still thought it was possible to go beyond the seemingly impossible to find once again the kernels of what was possible, what was real.

Annie didn't believe that any more. But was there any reason why she should?

Six months later I didn't know whether I believed it any more either. Two more disappointments with men, and another revival of my feeling that it was just too hard to get them to do the simplest things, the things that, as a woman, I took for granted. Anatomy might be destiny, but I had always been in revolt against destiny.

One evening, shortly after I had cried with despair over the futility of trying to love men, I met a friend for dinner. Suddenly, unexpectedly, there was a new element in our closeness. Every gesture was charged with an awareness of her sexuality in relation to my own. It was as if a floodgate had opened inside of me. My fantasies about making love with her bloomed like tropical flowers in the rainy season. So this was what it was like to desire a woman, I thought. And these things that I was imagining were the things that women did together . . . the things that we were going to do.

I hadn't planned it that way. I had no program for my life. There was just the intensity of feelings, the awareness that this was a woman I loved, a woman who loved me, a woman I could count on, a woman I could talk to about anything, a woman who understood me, and whom I understood. Now . . . well, there was something else.

I told her that I had never really kissed a woman, but that I wanted to. She said that she wanted to go to bed with me. I said I thought I wanted to but would be too scared. She said, "It's not really a question of genitals. It's just *wanting.* Wanting to be complete. And doing everything you can. There are all the same comforts and all the same frustrations."

"You know?" I said.

"Yes, I know."

Then we kissed each other. Everything was new. The kiss stood out in relief . . . because it had the significance that all kisses should have. There was nothing stylized or expected about it. There was everything shy and intense and fresh. Because no gestures between women could be assumed, every gesture was a beginning, something complete in itself. Her lips were very dry and chapped. She was embarrassed about it. We laughed. And hugged each other. The innocence of it was overwhelming.

Then we both went home to our own apartments.

Sometime later, we made love together. It was not everything. But it was not nothing either. At least we cared enough about each other that we were able to talk about the things that went wrong, the peculiar twists and turns of feeling, the fears, the hesitations, the doubts, the moments of self-recrimination, the moments of passion. We understood each other's bodies because they were our own bodies . . . we understood sensuality as well as sexuality. We were able to trust each other, sure in the knowledge that it was not a matter of conquest. There was too much to be overcome for that. We acted out of the fullness of caring, not the barrenness of ritual.

We searched out each other's needs, concentrating not so much on the sexual needs, but on the daily ones, sensing that the sexual could only be approached through the affirmations of daily living. We were gentle with each other, tolerant of each other, generous. We were also afraid . . . and willing to admit it. We learned the meaning of reassurance, the meaning of helping, of handling each other's insecurities as if they were items both fragile and precious. We learned how necessary it was to define our own personal boundaries, our capacities and incapacities, and to try to respect our own and each other's limitations. We struggled with the problems of overintensity and the problems of distance. We learned the subtle gestures that make of intimacy something secure. We learned that all of the weaknesses we had in our lives, we still had. We came to realize that it was no easier to love a woman than to love a man, that there was always the same potential for falling in love or getting hurt or being happy and unhappy, for hating and being scared, for small crises distorting into large ones, for expectations that spiraled beyond our capacities to fulfill them, for someone having power over you when you didn't want them to. We learned finally that we were just human beings . . . and flawed. We learned to respect those flaws and to comfort each other.

Comfort, I thought. That's what we need. All of us. Whether it's men and women or women and women. If only we could all learn to provide it.

One evening we were sitting in a popular New York bar. Out on the dance floor several couples were dancing together. Two heavy-set women, who out on the street would have been called butches, were holding each other tenderly. The expression in their eyes was as soft and loving as any woman's who is in love with a man. That expression transformed them as nothing else could, and made the "butch" designation seem impossibly cruel and distorted.

I remembered a discussion Annie and I had had one evening at the house in Maine. I had just come back from buying groceries, and had run into a homosexual couple on the street. Even though they were swishy, and I couldn't stand the parody of femininity that their mincing represented, I was still feeling warm and friendly toward the world in general. So I smiled at them. They glared at me. Their look was utterly contemptuous.

Sitting at the kitchen table, I said to Annie, "I just ran into a couple of faggots downtown—" Before I could finish the sentence, a jar of marmalade hit me in the stomach.

"Don't call them that," she said.

"Why not?" I asked. "That's what they are. It has nothing to do with being homosexual. It's just their manner that I can't stand. That's what makes them faggots."

"You mean because they act 'feminine'? What's wrong with acting feminine?"

"They're not acting feminine. They're aping femininity. There's a difference."

"I don't see it."

"All right then. How do you feel about dykes?"

"I don't like them."

"I do a lot of the time. But why don't you?"

"Because if I'm attracted to a woman, it's because she's a woman and not because she acts like a pseudo-man and has all of the characteristics I can't stand in men."

"So? Isn't that the same thing?"

"Maybe. I don't know."

I looked at the "dykes." They were big women. But they weren't hard. Or tough. I looked at my friend. She was tiny, small-boned. I knew that I too was attracted to a woman because she was like a woman . . . but a strong, vital, alive woman. Still, it was easy to see what the dykes found attractive in each other . . . the look of appreciation of what each authentically was, said it.

Watching them, my attention was suddenly distracted by loud laughter. It was coming from a table on the other side of the room. Eight women were sitting there . . . seven of them with cropped hair and crude, boisterous voices. The eighth looked like the commercial version of Miss America, a stewardess perhaps, with long, lacquered blonde hair and a 36-24-36 body. She was wearing a gray jump suit which clung to her from shoulder to ankle. When she spoke, it was in a high-pitched, babyish voice. All of the other women were vying for her attention. She was the choice piece of meat for the evening. One after the other, they asked her to dance, and I watched each of them run her hands over her body with sensuous, practiced skill.

There wasn't a trace of tenderness in anyone's expression. The jukebox was blasting out "Play It Funky" when Miss America's partner tossed a ten dollar bill onto the floor. The stewardess looked at it, giggled, shimmied provocatively and dropped into a crouch, her pelvis moving closer and closer to the floor until finally her crotch touched the bill. There was a roar of applause and approval from the women at the table.

I got up from the table. So this was liberation? Women treating each other in the same way that so many men had treated them? Women cheapening themselves, vulgarizing their own lives?

I couldn't stand to watch any more, so the two of us

picked up our drinks and moved over to the bar. Soon we were deep into an intimate, low-voiced conversation, my friend talking about experiences she'd had with a man she once loved. I was listening intently when a young man who had been standing nearby came over and asked me to dance. I refused. He asked my friend and she accepted. As she stood up and walked in front of him, he reached out and lightly, casually, touched my breast. It was too casual for me to say anything, but it made me feel slightly sick. Then, from across the room, I heard a homosexual man yell contemptuously at a lesbian woman, "Baby, you're just a cunt!" I wanted to cover my ears, to flee, but something in me insisted on absorbing everything that was happening, absorbing so that I wouldn't ever again allow myself to idealize either women *or* men, so that the reality would be clear to me, even if that reality was revolting.

Five minutes later my friend was back. Her partner had asked her if the two of us wanted to go to his apartment with him. She was not really surprised. I told her about his touching my breast. I was quietly shocked. "You're more optimistic about people than I am," she said. "That's the way most of them *are.*"

The thought depressed me, but I was more concerned with her than with everyone else, so we ordered another round of drinks and sat talking again, completely absorbed in each other. I can't remember precisely what we were saying, but I know that we were talking about something that touched both of our lives. Our heads were bent close together, but physically we were scarcely touching. I think I might have kissed her once or twice and brushed her hair back when it fell across her face. That was all. That must have been enough, because she was in the middle of a sentence when the woman behind the bar, a Nordic, conventionally pretty blonde, came over to us to interrupt. "Hey, you two, cut the heavy stuff," she said. "If you have to do that, go on home."

Do what, I thought? What had we been doing? Talking. Talking like two women who were genuinely interested in what the other had to say. Talking intensely. Touching tentatively, but with authentic concern . . . with affection.

I didn't want to stay any longer. The two of us stood up, paid the bill, and got our coats. As we started out the door, the woman behind the bar said to me, "Take care of the kid, will you."

I nodded miserably and walked out. I was on the verge of tears. Why did everything have to be so standardized, I thought. Was I the "masculine" one in this relationship? If so, then who would take care of me? But I *wasn't* the masculine one. Neither was I the feminine one. I was just a person. My friend was just a person. Wasn't that enough? Did everything have to fit into a prepackaged format? Why wasn't it possible to simply be oneself?

I thought of something Annie had said when she was feeling depressed about the problems of intimacy with women: "What are we going to do if it turns out that women are just as fucked up as men?"

I didn't have an answer then. Nor do I have one now. But I thought about the crew of seven and their "prize." *They* hadn't been told to cut the "heavy" activity. *We* had. Their behavior was acceptable. Ours wasn't.

Even among lesbians, then, there was a set of rules, standards about what constituted social and antisocial behavior. Those rules had nothing to do with sex . . . they had to do with exposure and authenticity. They had to do with the kinds of feelings it was permissible to express. Anything that stumbled across the boundaries of self-conscious control was taboo. Anything intense. Anything personal, immediate, anything that cut through the masks, the superficial layering of experience. Sex could always be depersonalized and stylized, made to fit into a slot, converted into entertainment. Love, because it was unpredictable, because it transcended every rule ever devised by human beings intent on hiding the evidence of their own vulnerability, their own nakedness, would always be subversive. If it was real, then it was unique—and threatening.

When my friend and I were out on the street, I kept my hands jammed into my pockets. It was hard for me to look at her. I felt very alone.

LOVE

"My chief occupation, despite appearances, has always been love. I have a romantic soul, and have always had considerable trouble interesting it in something else."

ALBERT CAMUS, *Notebooks: 1942–1951*

"People are getting killed, so who cares if John gets Mary in the end."

GRACE SLICK

I read *Anna Karenina* when I was sixteen. I didn't hear of Grace Slick until I was twenty-five. Somewhere between the two of them, my life and the life of my generation lies—with our expectations, beliefs, and behavior shaped by the nineteenth century values of our parents, our sense of defensive necessities shaped by the clash of romanticism and vulgarity in the fifties, and our adult life (what there has been of it) lived out in the egalitarian antiromanticism of the sixties, when every pattern of existence that I had struggled to adapt to, promptly became obsolete and was replaced by its near opposite.

I am of that generation that was brought up to believe that women had very special emotional needs, that love was always, or almost always, a more significant or more encompassing experience for a woman than for a man, and that, because of the dichotomies between men and women, it was necessary to protect women against the ravishments of male sexuality. I was taught: women love, men screw; save yourself for marriage; taught: don't squander your inner resources on someone who will only smash them; taught: men have affairs, women don't (although it was never clear with whom those men were having affairs if not women, since no one assumed they were having them with men); taught: men respect a woman who can say no; men want to marry virgins; taught: if you do what Anna Karenina did, you'll wind up where she wound up, dead on the railroad tracks. The moral of the story was: don't let your passions (if you have passions) run away with you. It can only lead to a bad end.

By the time I reached the age to apply any of these standards, however, the standards had changed. Women were supposed to be "equal" to men. That meant that being a virgin was nonsense, and having affairs wasn't. I was sixteen in 1960. My friends were becoming emancipated. Girls in my class at college spent whole evenings talking about whether or not to "give" their virginity to the boys they were going out with. Boys, in the spirit of true equality, offered to take it. By the time a girl was a sophomore, she wasn't supposed to be a virgin any more. True to the tone of the times, I wasn't. But two years later, I had a long talk with a male friend, three years older than I, who was planning to get married. He, as I, had always said that the idea of virginity was anachronistic. Except now, as he talked, he admitted that his prospective wife was a virgin, one of the few he had met, and said that it really meant something to him. I was astonished. And retrenched to think things over.

That was in 1963. A year or two later, I was no longer concerned about whether or not men wanted to marry virgins. What I was more concerned about was that some collision between the past and the present was taking place. "Egalitarianism" notwithstanding, women, including myself, were having a hard time being casual about the relationship between love and sex. Having decided that promiscuity wasn't a dirty word any more, our physical needs were still constantly being challenged by our emotional needs. Those of us who were trying to be free and committed at the same time discovered that perhaps this was a schizophrenic proposition. So was trying to be both romantic and practical. With Anna Karenina still hovering around the corners of my brain, I attempted the adaptation, coming to the "sensible" and "emancipated" conclusion that dating and Victorianism were idiotic. Daily life and sex, I decided, had to be blended carefully together. "Love" was something that you created and built. It did not just "happen."

Conceptually, of course, that was fine. Except even though it did not "just happen," it kept on happening. Having concluded that trial marriages were the only way to find out whether you could work things out with a man, it never occurred to me that a trial marriage might not succeed, that affairs might end, that love might die, not on the railroad tracks, but in arguments that were supposed to be settled by making love, or in resolutions about "freedom" and "nonpossessiveness," which tore the very heart out of intimacy. For years I had an upward and onward view of life, believing that growth inevitably led to more growth. Living with someone, I thought, was supposed to make you love each other even more.

I discovered that I was wrong. There were a number of things I hadn't counted on, things which none of my friends who wanted to be "free" had counted on. The first of these was that my attachments to men usually deepened the longer I knew them, and the more I shared with them, whereas their attachments seemed to lessen. The second was that when love didn't turn out as planned, there was some peculiar pain that I refused to acknowledge, a pain of separation that had not been part of the design. There was love and there was hate. Even though being emancipated meant being willing to take chances with your life, it also meant you might take chances that sent you reeling when you lost. I had never even thought about things like the "odds of winning" and "the price of losing." All I'd thought about was following my heart through a mystical wonderland where body, mind, and spirit joined in some perfect apotheosis fired by the good old puritan work ethic.

The other thing I didn't count on was the power of sex. I didn't realize that sex made a difference, or at least made that *kind* of a difference. I thought sex was an expression of love, a part of love. What I didn't think was that it transformed everything, that for me and for most women, making love with a man several times created unpredictable bonds—which weren't broken by saying: "THIS WAS A TRIAL MARRIAGE FOR WHICH THE CONTRACT HAS EXPIRED." I didn't realize that intimacy, physical intimacy, had unknown properties, that it created deepening needs, created highly unprogressive bursts of possessiveness and jealousy, created some balance between tension and satisfaction that became the mirror of every other aspect of a relationship. I didn't realize that sex deepened love and love deepened sex, even when love was on its way out. I didn't realize that love could reverse itself, could be withdrawn, or that the consequences of such a withdrawal could be so powerful as to crush vast expanses of one's own potential for feeling. I didn't realize there actually was such a thing as falling apart over the loss of love, nor that the difference between waking up next to a man you loved and not waking up next to him could be all the difference in the world.

What I discovered in the midst of my drive toward emancipation was that sex, love, hurt, and hate were the real stuff I was made of; that fairness, rationality, and the willingness to share or give away what one had never been sure of possessing in the first place, were all secondary characteristics, carefully cultivated to be sure, but capable of collapsing the moment stronger passions reared their heads.

Institutionalized monogamy might be an idea foisted on us by a property-oriented society, but when the person you loved stopped loving you, or you stopped loving someone, the idea of shifting over to someone else as if it represented no more than a change from Wheaties to Cornflakes seemed like a terribly cruel practical joke.

If Victorian society decreed that enjoying sex was taboo for women, and enlightened society decreed that women were entitled to as much pleasure in sex as men were, then "liberated" society decreed that sex and even exclusive love were oppressive to women. The seventies interpretation of "women's place" made the emancipation I had struggled (and never succeeded) to achieve a symbol of sexism. The loves I'd committed myself to were part of a male-dominated, Hollywood plot. Sex between men and women was pure exploitation. I was a creation of Madison Avenue.

Suddenly I wanted to scream . . . for God's sake just *stop.* Let me off this idiot merry-go-round. My psyche is not an ideological playground. My inner feelings, at their most genuine, are not ruled by social decree. You can have a thousand lovers if you want or have none. You can be a lesbian, a virgin, a career woman, a mother, or all four. But don't tell me who I am, or who it's best for me to be. You are right that A is true. But B and C and D are also true. Sandwiched in between three different mind sets, three different standards of "absolute right," I sometimes feel like a white rat being subjected to behavioral research with the data constantly being reevaluated. I recognize parts of myself when you speak of "women," but other parts don't fit the formula. I recognize parts of the males I know when you speak of men, but other parts defy categorization. I can't make the transitions required to fit the current theories of the age, especially since the ages are so telescoped that one barely has time to absorb one set of perspectives before another is all the rage. I don't know who women are. I scarcely even know who I am.

The rational mind is capable of making astounding leaps. I can espouse communism one evening and radical conservatism the next. I can theorize about the future of the family from dusk until dawn. I can create and destroy whole new systems of thought, systems of being, systems of living, all within the course of a dinner conversation. Similarly, I can create and re-create "new women" to suit the perspectives of the period. What I cannot do, however, is *become* the person each decade newly assumes I ought to be. I cannot be the completely feminine woman of the fifties, the emancipated, sexually free woman of the sixties, and the militant, antisexist woman of the seventies. I cannot ignore the fact that my own life has unfolded slowly, that it has been a part of all of those trends and none of them. I cannot ignore the fact that essentially the same me has persisted throughout the upheavals, throughout the analyses of historical circumstances and evaluations of what a woman's life ought to be.

The woman I've continued to be is a contradictory and uncertain human being. Believing in love, I am also terrified of it. Believing in stability, I live a thoroughly unstable life. Believing in marriage, I have never risked it. I am occasionally attracted to men exclusively on the basis of their sexuality, but am appalled when they are attracted to me on the basis of mine. I care about affection and doubt my capacities for it. I fantasize about conducting five love affairs simultaneously while living in sexless seclusion for long periods of time. I say friendship is superior to passion even as my throat is locking with the effort to suppress the effects of my latest passion. I long for liberation and don't know what it is. I hate when I would prefer to love and love when I would prefer to hate. The woman I am remembers a time in our not-so-remote history when American women (myself included) were objecting to the fact that American men were not as virile or gallant as their European counterparts; remembers when no self-respecting Jewish girl wanted to have anything to do with "nice Jewish boys." The woman I am knows that when I meet a man who is kind but sexless, my interest ebbs; that when I meet a man who is less than kind but sexually attractive, there is a struggle; that when I meet a man who is kind *and* sexually attractive, I am afraid of falling in love. My needs, fears, and desires remain as part of my daily life. The model of a liberated woman often fades into obscurity. And I am forced instead to confront a person . . . merely a person.

Like most other persons, I think I know what I want, but haven't the vaguest idea of how to go about getting it. A step at a time is about all I can manage. During one period of my life I became so accustomed to the problems of aborted love that I didn't know how to cope with the problem of its absence. Then I became so accustomed to the problems of love's absence, to the problems of isolation and solitude, that the mere thought of surrendering that isolation, allowing hopes long buried to materialize or crystallize, allowing myself to rely on another person and simultaneously face the possibility of isolation once again, made me take three steps backward to reconsider the question. My defenses were all neatly stacked on the side of solitude . . . but for love I had none. From time to time the need for love became stronger than the fear of it, and, despite my anxiety, my backlog of expectations and my memories of previous disasters, I would take the risk, though not with the greatest of ease. Now I am beginning to adapt to the presence of man-hating and lesbianism in my life, though I know that is hardly the end of the story. Sooner or later, I will try again . . . I will be a modified person, but not a wholly changed one.

At this point, however, distortion and mistrust have wormed their way deeply enough into my mind that I frequently feel stripped of the most fundamental clarity. I have seen use and abuse so often masquerading as love that more often than not I find it impossible to discern the true outlines of a fellow human being even in my most intimate encounters with men. Nothing can be relied upon to be itself. No gesture exists in a pure state, unaffected by a history that all too often has been a matter of standardized but nonetheless convincing performance. The fear of having my best impulses returned with a polite thank-you note or trampled on in all carelessness is sometimes overwhelming. I know that underneath the forms men and women have adopted to appease each other's sense of what we ought to feel and be, we are fundamentally the same (the same most of all in our fear of each other and our need), yet what I perceive, sometimes only half-consciously, is an alien and hostile being, whose authenticity cannot be assumed but must instead be proven.

It is as if, over the years, men have succeeded in digging such large holes in my sensibility that nothing any longer can be a matter of mere surfaces. Things drop straight to the bottom, tumbling past a familiar landscape in which all of the signs and symbols seem to have been already predetermined.

And yet . . . the power that love has over my life, whether by its presence or its absence, endures, and some conviction persists that it might be possible to find a way through the morass of mistrust and inauthenticity to something genuine, something real, something that does not wholly abandon the ideal. The conviction need not be stated, may even be emphatically denied, but still, in subterranean chambers of the spirit, it continues to hold sway—a final resistance launched by an internal aristocracy against the grayness of what is logical and reasonable to expect of life.

There are times, of course, when the cumulative weight of one's own failures and other people's failures is enough to make one renounce love entirely, at least insofar as that is possible. If love doesn't live up to the ideal, as it usually doesn't, then we conclude that the ideal is worthless. So we launch one experiment after another in alternative love styles, all of which prove to be as burdened with contradictions as more conventional styles, a fact that we struggle to ignore. It is not the style that counts, though, it is our capacity to transcend style for the sake of more permanent values. But in the general hullabaloo about what love should or could be, an enormous number of us have become trapped in an ersatz progressivism, becoming ashamed or embarrassed that ordinary love, with all of its attendant passions, still continues to be such an insistent and complicated force in our lives, over which we have little or no control.

Anyone, of course, can talk about sex, contemporary sex, technical sex. Anyone can have a discussion at the dinner table about the nature of orgasms. The word "fellatio" scarcely even merits a pause in the conversation. But love? Well that's something else again. That's a craw.

It's so much easier to say love is bullshit than to get over a love affair, so much easier to speak of oppression than to confess to private pain, so much easier in the long run to hate men than to love them. For when all of the speeches are done, there still isn't a man in bed next to you, no matter whether you believe in love or not. Love, fortunately or unfortunately, doesn't require our belief.

When Grace Slick said, "People are getting killed, so who cares if John gets Mary in the end," I wanted to agree with her, even though basically I knew that no matter how important deaths all over the world were, lives and loves were no less important. I wanted to agree but couldn't, and was aware that a great many people with intelligence, sophistication, and social conscience were as ashamed as I to confess to the "obsolete weakness" of caring about loving and being loved at least as much as they cared about the rest of the world. We would rather talk about anything than admit that learning to agree with Grace Slick is like learning that liver is good for you: the mind concedes while the stomach revolts.

None of my friends and none of their friends, no matter how many interests or commitments they have to the world of action and ideas, are capable of sailing off into the airy brightness of a concluded love affair. Certainly I am not. Inevitably there are consequences, both internal and external. If bodies are being killed all over the world because of politics rather than love, spirits are being smashed right next door, in apartment houses and shacks and on the street because of love rather than politics . . . love that can't—no matter how hard we try—be reinterpreted to fit *any* political mold, not even the mold of female oppression.

Of course, nowadays we see through the myths about love; we are cynical about the possible outcomes of relationships; we say, let's try to have relationships that are free of romantic poison, free of jealousy and possessiveness, which are generous, understanding, truly open.

What we do not say, however, is that despite our struggles with all of the important questions, despite our belief in freedom for nations and individuals, we have become so boxed into our circumlocutions about love that we admit only reluctantly the bald fact that whatever it is, we still need it. When all of the remedies and all of the rhetorical armor have been dropped, the absence of love in our lives is what makes them seem raw and unfinished. Personal hatred and personal fear destroy our capacities for loving more thoroughly than any social system possibly could. What we do not say is that love brings us face to face with the barest skeletons of our being. What we do not say is that we are all, every last one of us, scared of love's power to create and destroy.

Most of us at this stage of things aren't even sure of what we mean when we talk about love. If "real love" is simply a matter of placid, mutual contentment, why does the thought of a seemingly sexless union chill us to the bone?

We want to love people who are "good for us" and find that sometimes we love people who are not. Then we say that it probably wasn't love in the first place, but masochism. We want to combine the sensible and the impassioned, but when one or the other is missing (as they so often seem to be), we conclude that this must not be the real thing. The real thing, perhaps, is something that people who have lived together and compromised together and struggled together for twenty-five years or more know about—if their sense of affection and respect for each other has endured all of that time, if they are still capable of seeing each other freshly . . . but we have so few examples of that kind of attachment that we can scarcely turn to them for help. Perhaps it is something that people who have never lived together or only occasionally lived together know the most about. Perhaps it is something that emerges when two people who have been brought together by the good sense of their families discover what it is they have in common and pursue that commonalty in the lowest of keys. Perhaps it is the finale of *Tristan und Isolde.*

Whatever it is, most of us know very little about it. We can turn outward for evidence, to the world, and we can turn inward, to ourselves, for the evidence supplied by our own impulses, our own experiences.

The moment we turn outward, however, we are overwhelmed by the scarcity of available models. Since most of us are either unliberated and unhappy or liberated and unhappy, we look for people who are both happy and liberated. If our own lives are enough to make us abandon hope, we look to the lives of others for at least a vicarious sense of possibility. What we find, however, is usually nothing.

My aunt recently said to me, "You want too much. You aren't willing to compromise. Men will never be as sensitive or aware as women are. It's just not in their natures. So you have to get used to that, and be satisfied with something else."

"What else?"

"Either sexual satisfaction or theoretical intelligence or being loved and *not* understood or else being left alone to do the things you want to do."

"But those aren't enough."

"They have to be."

"Then I'd rather do without love altogether."

"You'll have to."

My aunt is fifty-five years old. She has learned the meaning of compromise. But how can I possibly compromise on things like warmth, communication, a passionate sense of life, a healthy capacity for commitment to the requirements of intimacy as well as to an outside purpose? I don't want to compromise on those things even if my aunt *is* right about the limitations of masculine "nature" (and I think she's wrong). Why should anyone compromise on whatever makes love worthwhile for them in the first place? And yet, even as she was talking, I thought that maybe she was right in this respect, maybe I did expect too much, the chief indicator being that, for the present, I *was* doing without love altogether . . . although as far as I could tell, that wasn't the reason, since I had, despite all of my criteria, always fallen in love with people, not characteristics, people who, although they did in fact possess those traits, possessed some very contradictory ones as well. (I shied away from the complicating thought that there were a whole slew of qualities on which I would prefer not to compromise in the future: integrity, sense of humor, humane intelligence, eccentricity, wildness . . . not even considering that my attractions were determined by less definable though equally potent impulses, so that there was room, alongside of my real life loves, for such figures as Robert Lowell, Muhammad Ali, and Norman Mailer, as well as Albert Camus and Dashiell Hammett, even though Camus and Hammett both happened to be dead.) What I wanted, finally, or so I thought, was someone I could enjoy being with as much as I enjoyed being with myself. A narcissistic notion, admittedly, and wide open to criticism, since even if I cannot quite forgive my own weaknesses, I at least know how to live with them and cannot say the same about someone else's weaknesses. All of these thoughts succeeded in driving me back in on myself, to a critique of my misplaced idealism, my stubbornness and "inflexibility," my unwillingness to adapt to "reality," the all or nothing quality of my attachments. If my aunt was right, though, then why hadn't her life been any happier than mine? The question gave me a headache, and I finally left the house, foundering in a sense of ultimate ambiguities.

Despite the headache, however, I was still aware that there are women who see things differently than my aunt does. I was also aware that women who are tough enough that they have not needed to expunge softness from their lives, and soft enough that they have not needed to expunge toughness, women who work and love and are loved in return (loved in whatever ways they need to be loved), function out there in the world, since from time to time one or another of them raises a voice. I am profoundly curious about such women, although it is usually difficult for me to get anything more than a glimpse of their lives in action, particularly if they are somewhat older than myself. My own experience has always been that as a young, unmarried woman, contact with middle-aged married women together with their husbands is in itself so fraught with danger and insecurity that every exposure becomes a matter of ultimate, diplomatic delicacy, revealing finally that no matter how happy or liberated Mrs. Wholly Integrated Life is, there is still some hidden nerve in her that goes taut from the strain of protecting her own turf while trying simultaneously not to reveal that she feels any need to protect it. More often than not, I have found it necessary to spend four hours talking with the wife to every five minutes I spent talking with the husband, and that if any warmth or communication or understanding was generated between me and the husband, I became automatically suspect, *even* at those times when I basically found the woman as interesting if not more interesting than the man. As Miss Wholly Unintegrated Life, then, I instantaneously fell into the class of threatening creatures, notwithstanding the argument that in order to regard Mrs. So-and-So as a worthwhile model, I would also want to regard her choice of partners as worthwhile. There is little space in the midst of all this porcupinage for earnest gropings after a woman with whom to identify, a man to admire, and pleas for understanding and tolerance. While usually engaging, the husbands (for other reasons) provoke little positive response from the wives, who seem to expect me to wade through their nightmares like a bitch in heat, trailing a terrible scent from her side of the bed over to his. Can I comfort such women and say, "I understand very well how you feel and would probably feel the same way in your place," when what I really need is some woman in whom I can see the model of a greater self-confidence than my own? I can't, and in all fairness to her, I would even have to admit that I have been involved more than once with a husband, but that I have never been involved with a happy husband, and, in fact, was so delighted on the few occasions that I have met one, that I far preferred to enjoy the light of his happiness than steal it away. It also, I am sure, would not help very much to confess that sometimes, after making love with someone's husband, we have talked about his wife, and that despite my frequent attacks of jealousy, there were times when I felt more sympathy and empathy for her than for him, since the things that disturbed or disappointed or irritated her about him were very often precisely the things that bothered me. (Sisterhood is found in strange places.) If that leaves my image tarnished, I can only say that I am more in search of truth than heroism anyway, and that my nervous system accommodates itself to the worst of situations as well as the best. What was sought was lost, in any event, and, given the perils of such peculiar camaraderie, the problem of finding older, married women as models remains, for the time being, unsolved.

If I get back to the original model, the one who finally is all important, and from whom the other models of necessity derive—my mother—there is little in the way of comfort or insight that can be gained. As a child in Russia she was considered so fragile that she was expected to spend her days lying in a hammock resting. As a wife, she was expected to be a beautiful and charming doll. As a mother, she wished for a daughter who would also be a doll. It was expected that in line with middle class European standards, she would have a governess to take care of the house and the children, that she would never hold a job, and that she would spend her evenings waiting for her husband. What she should *do* with her life was *think* about the needs of her family, get a lot of sleep, and go to the beauty parlor once a week. Not knowing how else to use up her energies, she became a compulsive shopper, going from one department store to another, buying and exchanging, buying and exchanging, even at those times when she had so little money that almost everything had to be returned. She is exquisitely sensitive, high-strung as a hummingbird, and so insecure that she has to telephone my father five times in the course of a day to resolve the question of what she should prepare for dinner. She possesses an enormous wealth of untapped strength, and since no one ever provided channels for that strength, she is in a constant state of nervous paralysis . . . terribly afraid of life . . . afraid for our lives as much as for her own. She lies awake at night, transforming our worlds into disaster areas from which she should be clearing the rubble, imagining fatalities in every street crossing, sure that we will not survive from one breath to the next. And yet . . . in a crisis she has more strength than any of us, can cope with gargantuan problems, carry enormous packages up six flights of stairs, understand the subtle problems of my father's business affairs (but only at those times when he can't understand them and literally *has* to be helped), drive six hundred miles in the course of a day to deliver a car for him, and cook twelve courses in one evening to feed fifty people, even though at other times she is so "inefficient" about cleaning the house that the dishes sit in the sink for up to twenty-four hours. She's not really inefficient or incompetent. She's miserably unhappy, and doesn't know that the lack of an independent focus to her life has turned all of her best impulses destructively inward.

I love her but I can't look to her for an example. I wish she were happier, but despite that wish, I still have to struggle against all of those impulses of doubt and insecurity (I leave the dishes for four days) that she has passed on to me, have to create myself in my own image rather than hers.

Elsewhere, the prospects are not much more reassuring. I can scrounge around and come up with a handful of women writers who spent a good deal of their lives in open revolt against their condition: George Eliot and Virginia Woolf and Doris Lessing and Simone de Beauvoir and Sylvia Plath in particular, whose work I admire at least as much as the fact that they are "women writers." But the lives and loves of women writers have not been notoriously successful (writers are a neurotic breed to begin with): Doris Lessing lives alone; Sylvia Plath and Virginia Woolf both committed suicide, although at very different stages of their lives; and Simone de Beauvoir questioned—when it was too late to change things—whether she hadn't made a crucial mistake in not having any children. George Eliot fared a good deal better than the others. She and the married Lewes lived together for many years, until his death; from all accounts, they lived happily, or as close to happily as human beings can.

None of them, however, successfully combined marriage *and* children and working, which is what I and many of my friends would like to do. But even if *all* of them had led superbly balanced lives, fulfilling every aspect of their personal and biological destinies, three or four literary models are not very much to go by (those who seek male writers for models have a large enough selection that sooner or later they're bound to find someone with whom they can identify, both personally and artistically). The result of all this, for me at least, is the reluctant conclusion that whatever I become and whatever ways of loving I find will have to be the product of a union between frequently blind struggle and sheer luck.

I do not know many women who spend their lives waiting for phone calls or cleaning out ashtrays or wondering frantically what they are going to do on a Saturday night. I do, however, know a great many women who are active, sensitive, and intelligent, women for whom the achievement of "liberation" was a goal long before it became part of a crusade, a goal created by inner necessity rather than popular concern. There was no choice for them except to struggle to be themselves, simply because it took too much out of them to go by the rules. It is precisely those women who are currently in the worst predicament, stranded on the outer edges of the movement, increasingly isolated and frustrated. In the past several months, four men I like and respect said to me on separate occasions that they missed having worthwhile male companionship. "The most interesting people around are all women," they said.

It was true, I thought, that there seemed to be a shortage of male counterparts. I too was unhappy about the flaccidity, the one-dimensionality, the lack of imagination, the lack of life in most of the men I saw around me. Where was their energy, their activity, their spontaneity? Where was their passion? The women I knew were filled with passion, not only sexual passion, although that too, but the passion for seizing life and shaping it, infusing it with the breath of an expansive humanity, an intelligent vitality. And they were gagging from the effort of repressing their desire for a truly human form of love.

What are we freeing ourselves *for,* I thought, if not to become happier people? What use is it to liberate one's potential if there is no one capable of valuing or matching or responding to that potential?

None of us can go back to the old images of domestic bliss . . . we were revolting against that long before we had any coherent sense of why we were doing it. We worked to create ourselves, and then looked for male co-creators. We wanted so badly to be "finished women" first. But the struggle to become self-reliant cost us so much, required so much hard labor and produced such tentative gains that it sometimes seemed we would never succeed in overcoming our own psychic entropy, never be complete. Yes, we wanted to sharpen our minds on the daily clashes of alive intellects. Yes, we wanted our days to be rich in exposures to a kaleidoscopic, outside world. Yes, we wanted to be proud of our strength. But no, we never wanted to become worthy of the pedestal, the icy heights of achievement. We wanted love that was intense but not consuming. We wanted to be cared for, thought of, and valued, not abstractly, as men often value women, but in the accumulation of daily minutiae that make life dense and intricate and worthy of infinite consideration. We were seeking in men what we were seeking in ourselves, a combination of strength, diversity, commitment, passion, and sensitivity . . . seeking an equivalent humanity.

Where are we now, though, having tested and experimented and explored the possibilities? Most of us, I think, are stuck, not knowing what the next step is, aware that we have stumbled upon a complexity we would never have dreamed existed: having increased our expectations, we have also increased our disappointments; having taken the risks, we are feeling the consequences.

A lot of us are desperate. A lot of us are scared. Of the women I know, a few are basically alone and trying to come to terms with that; a few have been trying to build love and are discovering that they can't even find the materials for an adequate foundation; a few have committed themselves to the complexities and uncertainties and satisfactions of loving other women; a few are paralyzed by their desires for marriages and families since they can't figure out how to blend responsible wifehood, motherhood, and careerhood; and a few are so afraid of asking anything at all from love any more, of losing control over their fetal, liberated selves, and wanting something they have become convinced they will never get, that they would rather not fall in love at all.

In the process of attempting to become "separate individuals" many of us have had to anesthetize ourselves to needs that are nonetheless real and deep. We have rationalized our desires for love and affection, permanence and stability, equating those desires with a capitulation to unresolved weakness in ourselves. Trying to keep up with the demands of the world, with the expectations of men and ourselves, with "contemporary" modes of behavior, we have lost touch with much of what we really want. The moment we regain contact with ourselves, there is a flinching away. Why want what we can't have anyway, we say, and return to the fray.

But spreading ourselves around, we discover that there is some thinness in our intimacies that leaves hollow spaces inside of us. Trying to be undemanding and independent, we discover that we are engaging in a new form of self-sabotage. Concentrating our energies on one person, we're fearful of being overly vulnerable to the effects a single relationship can have on us. As it turns out, we are too real to bear the weight of our own theories.

Life is a never-ending seesaw of possibilities in which, more often than not, we are forced to conclude that no matter what we do to adapt, we still wind up sitting on the side that is up in the air. Very few women (very few people at all) come out of the struggle to shape and adapt (particularly when they haven't figured out yet what they want to shape or adapt to) without feeling the edge of desperation and incompletion grinding at their teeth, without feeling the terrible uncertainty, the terrible doubt about whether they will succeed in coming out of it whole. And, meanwhile, the nagging questions remain: do I, perhaps, need too much? . . . do I need . . . well, anything? . . . how much is too much? . . . how little is nothing? And where, in all this chaos of construction, do I, exhibit A, one human being, fit in?

The same problems are always recurring. They have to do with dependency and immobilization, sex and affection, permanence, continuity, and fidelity. There was a time in my life when I swore that I would never get married, never be "chained" to another human being, never allow myself to depend on any person other than myself, never try to inhibit a man in the pursuit of his freedom, never demand anything at all, least of all fidelity. Happiness, I thought, lay in the commitment to freedom. When my mother said, "You can't have love affairs the rest of your life. Look what happens when they end," I answered with, "Oh mother, don't be ridiculous. I have a life of my own. I have my work, my friends, my freedom." Having drawn such a blueprint for what my happiness ought to consist of, I eventually wound up with a near nervous breakdown when the effort to live within the drawing's dotted line proved to be too much for my still renegade psyche. If my mother's design was a failure, mine certainly wasn't a success.

The breakdown cost me a lot, but it also taught me a lot . . . mainly that it is useless to design a life for yourself that you can't possibly live, and that the effort to determine what one really wants and needs is more complex and demanding than I would have thought—though also more worthy of attention.

The first contradictions I discovered in myself related to dependency and immobilization. Despite the fact that I could live alone for years at a time, support myself in banal as well as curious ways, travel alone all over the world, drive a motorcycle at seventy miles an hour, have sex with whomever I chose, I was still capable of sitting by a telephone, unable to think of anything beyond whether or not a man I loved was going to call and feeling the most common hurt and frustration when he didn't. I have known myself to spend hours or even days wandering around my apartment, uninterested in books or music or friends, uninterested in going anywhere or doing anything, simply because my imagination had made me believe that some slight quarrel with someone I loved or some excessive or inappropriate demand represented a prelude to the "final separation." I have heard the voice struggling to burst free inside of me, the voice that longs for a condition of life in which my every action and reaction would be regulated by me and no one else, the voice that demands a freedom which all too often seems hollow when it is achieved.

Certainly it was not a question of being liberated enough to make phone calls myself. I had made those calls many times. It was a question of security (a word I have always looked upon with contempt). No Female Bill of Rights could give me that kind of security. What I needed to know at those particular moments was whether it mattered enough to the man for him to do the calling. Yes, of course, I should have had more confidence, should have been able to say, "Well, if he doesn't care that much, the hell with him." Or, "Phone calls aren't so important." That is precisely what I *did* say. I grew furious at myself and spoke contemptuously of "neurotic need." I stiffened with resistance, swearing that "never again" would I allow that to happen. Hating myself for retaining these vestiges of insecurity, I struggled to raise my consciousness to such a high level that I might purchase immunity through it. The only thing I succeeded in doing was having such a high level of consciousness that I could look down on myself from my perch and call myself a fool and an idiot. In the long run, however, I accomplished precious little in terms of changing the way I felt.

"You should go out and get a job. Have something to occupy your time so that those things won't matter," someone might say. Except I already had a job, sometimes even two jobs. "Take a vacation," someone else might say. "Go away for a while." Except I would go away and would come back thinking that now I had a better perspective on things, only to spend the next night pacing the street in front of the apartment house where the man I loved lived, determined not to go inside because I didn't want to interfere with his privacy, his freedom, his self-determination, and so on, ad infinitum. Perspective, I soon realized, was a fine commodity, but utterly useless when I was in the thick of things. My "wisdom" deserted me; a crisis that should not have been a crisis became one anyway. Maybe he didn't want to be with me . . . maybe I should leave . . . why was he feeling so irritable . . . was it because of me . . . did he still love me . . . why couldn't I control the terrible trips my imagination went on? Why couldn't I be like my friend Marsha, who never seemed to be immobilized by such things herself, but who was constantly pursued by men who sat in front of telephones waiting for *her* to call, men who went away on vacations so as not to interfere with *her* privacy, her freedom, her self-determination. The horrifying absurdity of not being in control—ever—except when I wasn't in love, except when someone didn't really matter, scared me so much, I decided it was better not to love anyone at all. Wasn't it easier in the long run, to simply be alone? Yes it was . . . sometimes. But then at other times, well . . . something crunched inside of me at the thought. I might wrestle myself to the ground—but it was always I who lost.

Of course, I know that the fear of immobilization and the fact of immobilization are not unique to me. Disbelievers in love seem to be as susceptible to it as believers . . . liberationists as much as antiliberationists, homosexuals as well as heterosexuals, weathermen as much as construction workers and ghetto dwellers, corporation heads as much as junkies. It is one of the few phenomena that is still totally egalitarian, despite the inequities that are its breeding ground.

I don't even believe that such immobilization is a typical experience for women and an atypical one for men. I have seen too many men who were as happy or as demoralized as I, depending upon the current status of their intimate relations with women. Men and women usually love differently (and in general I think that women love in a more integrated way), but we all feel the same sense of seemingly excessive consequence when love doesn't turn out as we want it to, or when we are not what we thought we could be, or when love is simply absent from our lives. Our common isolation is so profound and our common needs so overwhelming that the meeting of the two almost invariably produces an awareness that we cannot possibly ask so much of our relations with another human being, but cannot ask any less, either. Very few of us, male or female, are secure enough to believe that the collapse of everything is not just around the corner, in the next phone conversation, the next night spent together, the next trip taken, all the more so since the odds, as we see them, are overwhelmingly against us.

Still, I have never been able to get over the secret twinges of sympathy, pity and contempt (fear's disguise) that mingled inside of me whenever I saw a woman suffering over love . . . pity and contempt because she was so exposed, because she made me feel so painfully aware of my own susceptibility to the same kind of exposure . . . sympathy because of the shared knowledge derived from similar experience. I remember once while waiting to use a pay telephone hearing the young woman who was talking inside the booth say, "Barry, please, are you coming? Please, just tell me, are you coming?" Barry's answer apparently wasn't affirmative because the woman then said, "Listen, I'll *pay* for the plane. I know it's a long drive. But I have the money. And I want you to come."

I couldn't stay around to hear the rest. Even the fragment of unsatisfied need made me cringe for her. And I wanted to run from the sound of her voice, so unhappy, so dependent, so desperate. In some sense, every woman who has ever been hurt by love (even through her own doing) is a mirror of myself, and I cannot stand to see that self . . . a self beyond the comforts of rationality or understanding . . . a self that resembles a child trying to walk and falling on its face at every third step. No one, of course, thinks that a child is ridiculous for falling on its face. What we think is that it's trying to walk. But when an adult face reveals that same look of astonishment, hurt, and bewilderment over having fallen, there is something in us that fights not to see, because it is so close to the look on the faces of people who are starving but also proud, a look at once haunted and fierce, half-disbelieving, half-naked, a look that expresses more than anything the helplessness felt by anyone trapped by seemingly unalterable conditions or circumstances.

Confronted with that look, an unbearable fury sometimes rises in reaction. I have felt that fury on behalf of my mother, and at her. There were times when I wanted to yell at her, "Stop suffering, just stop," because I didn't know what else to do, and couldn't stand the sight of it; times when I wanted to crucify my father for having contributed to that look, times when I wanted to say to them, "Please love each other . . . but decently." There is nothing more awful than seeing a person's capacity for love turned into a travesty of feeling.

Men frequently tell a joke about the woman who said, "no no no" when he touched her, and then refused to let go of him. You never hear a joke about a man in the same position. The joke is about the use and abuse of power, and in the woman's "no no yes yes," I see the core of a real dilemma. To many women (to me), the desire to reach out toward men, both physically and spiritually, is constantly being sabotaged by the fear of being psychologically mutilated. Many of us, I think, have turned against our own needs mostly because we've seen the price other women have had to pay for them. If it hurt me to see the woman in the phone booth needing Barry, then damn it, I was never going to need a Barry. If it hurt me to see my parents' marriage flounder in its own contradictions, then I would never marry, especially since the first word that entered my mind whenever I thought of marriage was divorce. If it hurt me to see women suffering over their husband's infidelities, then I was going to make absolutely sure that fidelity was unimportant. If the thought of living with someone and having them leave me made me physically ill, then I just wouldn't live with anyone . . . period. Those "free choices" I had told my mother about, were not, as it turned out, such free choices after all. They were choices made as a reaction to a need, not out of the need itself.

Of course, such tactics for dealing with one's own needs just don't work, since the needs remain, subterranean and pervasive, even as the fears of "slipping up" and accidentally surrendering to them, increase. You are left, finally, with nothing more nor less than yourself.

One of the problems that feeds immobilization among women, derives, I think, from the conflict between passivity and activity. Many of us (myself included) have been trained to the kind of passivity in relationships that makes us feel our own helplessness so much more acutely in situations that seem to require active behavior, and even when we do manage to overcome the passivity, we are often so uncertain about the "rightness" of it that we either vacillate from one to the other, or else require triple reinforcement from men. If I make one phone call, then he should make three. If I'm active, then he should be twice as active. If he turns out to be *less* active, the stage is set for a disaster. And in order to avert such disasters, our minds race forward to the questions, "What can I do to change myself," "how make it easier for him," "how give more," stalling finally at the thought, "But I've already given all I have." Since we can't do for him what we wish he would do, we grope for ways to excuse him or justify him. This ambivalence about actively asserting our needs, this hidden desire to have him assert our needs for us, this reluctance to articulate the nuances of caring that our imagination tells us are capable of transforming a relationship from something ordinary to something generous and spontaneous, puts us in an impossible bind: immobilized simply because we cannot take his place, cannot go through the mind-bending maneuvers of "chasing him until he catches us" without feeling ourselves go rigid from the effort of spanning the contradictions.

The idea of activity and passivity becomes an ironic joke from the moment one finally abandons the passive stance and is forced to realize that neither activity nor passivity can substitute for or camouflage the real work of love. I *cannot* make up with my own activity for a lack of activity on his part. I can make a dozen phone calls, but that changes very little if he feels like talking to me once a week and I feel like talking to him ten times a week. I can assert my right to be involved with several men, but that won't help me if I have no desire to exercise my "right" and he doesn't think of it as his "right" at all, but exercises it nonetheless. I can say, "let's live in the same apartment," but I can't change the fact that when he's there, he's only half there. I can say, "Why don't we take separate vacations," but if, in the end, my desire to be with him is stronger than my desire to take a separate vacation, it is *I* who will concede the point and not he. I can propose marriage, but I can't make him into a husband. On the other hand, I can state my opposition to marriage, with which he'll heartily agree, and then stew in the juice of my own confusion over whether I'm afraid of being trapped by permanence or really want it after all, while simultaneously realizing that no matter what I want, relationships aren't made permanent or impermanent by the act of marriage.

All in all I can be as active as I please and wind up with nothing more than I had during that period in our prehistory when women were supposed to be passive. That, I think, is the real issue. Not equal rights—but differing needs, differences that are accentuated by the fact that we usually choose to love people who are not precise reflections of ourselves and therefore, by definition, have differing needs from our own.

Which brings me to one of the most satisfying and most frustrating aspects of loving another woman. We look at each other, at the mirror images that our bodies return to us. Giving to each other, we are given the gift of ourselves; we become more complete human beings. The process is a healing one. I can help to cure the things in her that men were unable to cure in me. Not only is she as intense as I am, as active, as (or more) contradictory, as dependent upon similar needs (the need for small securities, small attentions, the need to express her emotions openly, to be unafraid of the consequences of doing that), but she is also a creature subject to the same biological laws and pressures as I am: the pains, the desires, the periodicities. She has a womb. She bleeds.

And yet, if some of the laws of biology make us conscious of bonds, others make us conscious of gaps. Desiring what is similar to myself, I also desire what is dissimilar. My body may be soothed, comforted, stimulated, satisfied, but ultimately I am forced to acknowledge the gap created once again by biology. It is a simple truth, but nonetheless a profound one. We both have spaces inside of us that are untouched in our most intimate exchanges.

The awareness of that can also be immobilizing. For if one kind of immobilization comes about the moment you sense that you are helpless to change a situation, that neither activity nor passivity means anything where there are differences in kind and degree of life requirements, then immobilization of another kind can also come about when you realize that as a woman existing in enduring biological relation to man, you cannot surrender those moments with a man that seem, in an instant, to be capable of redeeming all the rest.

Human beings are capable of convincing themselves of just about anything. One of the things we spend the most time trying to convince ourselves about is sex. Our convictions, we say, reflect the nature of our "needs" . . . except those needs change so often that it's hard to believe in their permanent nature. In the Victorian era it was thought that only men needed sex; decent women merely tolerated it but were incapable of enjoying it. Men, the crude beasts, had a stronger biological drive, and that meant that nearly every sexual encounter between a man and a woman was a form of civilized rape.

Then came Freud. Women, it seemed, needed sex too. In fact, whenever their natural sexual drive was thwarted, by guilt or anxiety, by an impotent husband or a puritanical society, an insensitive lover, an indifferent lover, or no lover at all, they ended up with symptoms: they became neurotic.

Once female sexuality had been officially sanctioned and even prescribed (no proper dosage was ever established), women, free now to confront the claims of biology just as men did, moved more openly into the bedrooms of the world. Many women had always done what they wanted to do in private, but now it was no longer a private matter at all, but a public one. People kept records of their sex lives, counted the number of orgasms they had, the number of partial coitions, the number of frustrations. Men timed their erections, trying to think about business appointments so that they might delay ejaculation long enough for the woman to catch up and share a—1950's fadeout, 1960's zoom in—perfect orgasm. Girls looked forward to college because they wouldn't be obliged to have sex under the football bleachers any more, but would be able to do it in their own beds (if their roommates were accommodating enough to leave during parietals). The best thing about having your own apartment was that you didn't have to make a man leave in the middle of the night.

In the seventies, women retrenched. A kind of neo-Victorianism began to take the place of the permissiveness that characterized the sixties. Once again, in the name of pseudo-liberation, people (this time it was the women themselves rather than the men) began to claim that it was impossible for a woman to enjoy sex with a man, tainted as it always was by the poison of sexist oppression. No allowances were made for sex that was not crude, sex infused with passionate warmth, sex that made you suddenly aware of what a fine thing it was to possess a body capable of expressing so many nuances of feeling.

If I was sick of hearing rave reviews on behalf of the sexual drive, sick of listening to people who celebrated how close we were to the animal kingdom and how much closer we could be if only we would live by our "instincts,"* I was equally sick of pompous pronouncements about female purity. If I refused to allow myself to be a victim of "oppression" I would also refuse to be a victim of Victorianism or the animal kingdom. What I wanted was—yes, sex—but sex with love, sex that expressed something more than *just* biology.

Several years ago, when I was hitchhiking through Greece, I was picked up by a Greek industrialist in a Mercedes Benz. He had been out hunting on his estate with a friend, and the two of them were on their way back to Athens. The car smelled of pipe tobacco and gun oil and quality leather. I liked it. I also liked the industrialist. It was dark out and I was sitting in the back seat, so I could scarcely see him, but I could hear his voice. It was the voice I liked especially: a rich, mellow, powerful voice. He and his friend laughed a lot, and their laughter was so wholesome and expansive that even though I couldn't

*It is a well known fact that throughout the animal kingdom female sexuality is strictly regulated by the laws of periodicity. Bitches in heat are available. The rest of the time they are untouchable. The male animal, subject to no such cycle, knows that he risks being mangled by an irate female if he oversteps the boundaries, and consequently, for his own protection, learns to respect those boundaries.

understand what they were talking about, I found myself laughing too. The ride was long, and after a while the industrialist, whose name was Costas, started talking to me in fractured though comprehensible English. I found more to like in him than his voice. His reckless abuse of the English language was enormously appealing, and he didn't hesitate to try and express complex thoughts with an "I see Jane, Jane sees me" vocabulary. He was more concerned with his own passion for expression than with the need for precision. He fired questions at me with complete disregard for my personal privacy, as if it were his right to ask whatever came into his head. He laughed at my answers, or was thoughtful, or asked more questions.

Hours later, he dropped off his friend in a fashionable Athenian suburb. When he opened the car door to let his friend get out, the interior light of the car shone on his face and on mine. His face matched his voice and his English.

I got into the front seat. The first thing he said was, "You no only intelligent. You attractive too." I would have returned the compliment, if I hadn't felt suddenly shy. Then he asked me if I would see him again. I said yes. He dropped me off at the youth hostel in Athens, took the phone number there, and drove back home to his family.

I expected not to hear from him again, but he called at eight in the morning. For the next week or so I spent my nights at the youth hostel and my days with him. He took off from work to show me everything in Athens. When he couldn't be with me, he insisted that an employee accompany me wherever I went and take care of my most minuscule need. I was embarrassed and said that I had traveled all over Europe with a knapsack on my back and no help from anyone, that I could manage perfectly well by myself. He insisted: I capitulated. We spent a great deal of time eating enormous meals and walking. I thoroughly enjoyed myself. I was very attracted to him, and assumed that sooner or later we would probably go to bed together. One afternoon we did, or rather almost did. Right in the middle of things, I jumped up off the bed and ran out of the room. I couldn't do it. I was attracted to him, but not in love with him. At the last instant, that was what counted. I was terribly ashamed of myself for having "tempted" him and then backed off. I tried to explain and couldn't. He, surprisingly, despite my inability to explain, understood anyway. I was very grateful to him for that. "It will happen," he said. "But slowly."

It never did happen, though. In a couple of weeks I wanted to be on my own again, to go off to an island with my knapsack and my sixty dollars. He said that I would need money on the island, that he would pay for a house and would also pay for an apartment in Athens if I would come to see him a few times a month. I should not be worried about money, he said. In fact, if I was willing, he would set up a fund for when I went back to America so I could go back to college and get an education. "With you intelligence, you need education," he said. I said thank you but no thank you. The prospect of being taken care of made me feel completely trapped and uncomfortable. Also, I remembered the afternoon in his apartment. I knew that the same thing would happen again the next time, that I wouldn't be able to do it.

So I packed up my things, said goodbye, and left on the next boat. We wrote letters back and forth for over a year. I still think of him with affection. When I fell in love with someone else, he was very happy for me.

I was sorry that sex had been a problem. But I have been familiar with another side of the coin too. Sometimes, when I was in love with a man, I became worried that once we got into bed, we would never get out of bed. My body vibrated all day long. If he was fifteen feet away from me in the same room, my vision blurred. I had to fight against a constant sense of sexual distraction. If we spent the day making love, I was angry at myself for being so susceptible to sex. If we spent the day doing something else, my imagination had us in bed anyway. Love and sex, it seemed, were a powerful combination.

A third side of the coin, or perhaps the edge between the sides: I have spent the past three years of my life in near complete chastity. The combined strains of having been treated too often as a piece of meat and having loved once too often proved finally to be too much for me. I couldn't sleep with someone I didn't love, and since I was afraid to love anyone, I slept alone. If I tried to sleep with someone I didn't love, I hated myself. If someone who didn't love me tried to sleep with me, I hated that person. In the long run it was best, perhaps, to do without. Whether it was best or not, it was the only thing I could do.

There are no easy reductions to be made as far as sex is concerned. The need certainly exists. Chemistry exists. But there are other needs that exist too. Our minds have to be satisfied as well as our bodies. Our dignity and sense of self-respect have to be maintained. We are creatures capable of making choices. Society may be responsible for oppression as well as Victorianism. Our parents may be responsible. But I am responsible for me, no matter who did what to whom over the past several thousand years.

It's true that sometimes an evening with three glasses of wine and a man I considered attractive has been enough to modify my needs so that I found myself in bed with him at the end of the evening. It is also true that when we finished making love, I couldn't understand what he was doing in my bed. I didn't want him to be there. When the sexual drive was exhausted, all that remained was a sense of the gap between sex and love.

That is not true of everyone. It is true of me.

One young woman recently admitted to me that sometimes if a man was good in bed, she preferred being with him to being with a man she respected more in other ways. Another woman I know picks up men on the street every once in a while. She doesn't know why she does it, and she hates herself for it. But still. . . . A third woman who never had any sexual interest in any man other than the man she loved, changed overnight as soon as they broke up. Suddenly she went to bed with a different man every night. If he paid for dinner, she repaid with sex. She also hated herself.

All of those ways of treating sex are, I think, derivative . . . or else part of a stage. Many women go through periods of promiscuity, when they're very young and are experimenting, or when they've just finished a love affair and are so miserable that they are trying to cover up their deepest feelings.

Still, the need for continuity, for love, for something with at least enough solidity to make permanence seem possible, even if it usually isn't attained, persists. No matter what our concepts of freedom are, there is no way to ignore the simple fact that it takes a long time to get to know people, to understand their strengths and weaknesses and coordinate them with your own, to balance the weight of closeness and separateness, to arrive at some degree of sexual openness. The prospect of repeating the process over and over again is exhausting, even for a fertile imagination.

Our bodies are shaped to the requirements of depth and space. A man's body literally moves into yours and somehow takes up residence there. Something is imbedded in the flesh . . . not immediately, but soon enough. It's not something you can wash off or douche away. There is some respect for process that is bred into us or is part of our sex more deeply than we ever planned it to be, and the corridors within us are never penetrated instantly. I cannot be warm and open with every man I meet who appears to me to be trustworthy (not even if I were less cautious and less skeptical). There is some dialogue of intimacy that builds itself up gradually, a dialogue that I wouldn't know how to violate and wouldn't wish to violate. Once that intimacy has been built, shaped, then its retraction involves some severance from yourself, that self that you slowly learned to share and communicate. There are deeply stamped patterns, rituals, habits, individually constructed, that do not make life boring at all. On the contrary, given the generally transient quality of our lives, they make it seem richer and more dense.

Hands, mouths, and genitals speak as loudly as voices. There is in them the articulation of everything that otherwise remains mute within us. They describe every arc of feeling of which we are capable. But within each relationship they describe something singular and personalized, something that can be translated only within the context of so many other aspects of being close to another human being. I cannot be free sexually with a man I don't know well or feel deeply for, partly because of simple reserve and partly because everything I have to say with my body takes a while to decipher. It takes unanticipated phone calls, made not out of duty, but out of affection (so many men seem to require a "reason" for phoning, never realizing that the gesture contains its own reason). It takes the accretion of experiences shared, whether that's the experience of sitting alone together in a room and doing very different things, or the experience of spending three days together in concentrated intensity, or the experience of seeing all of your defenses and affectations split off from you in a moment of unexpected closeness.

When all that is ignored, the effect is like dry ice tearing off a layer of skin.

Germaine Greer has suggested that we should all give ourselves, freely, easily, generously, has said that sex is fun, kissing is fun. Nothing mystical about it. But when she wrote, "The sensations caused by the two kisses,"—one that expresses love and one that doesn't—"are not genuinely distinguishable," perplexity descended on me. Was I deluded, I thought? Pretending? Obsolete? What was I to do with the fact that it had always been even harder for me to kiss someone I didn't love than to have intercourse with them? I know many other women for whom this is also true.

Kisses, I think, probably still bear the weight of our first experiences with love and tenderness from our parents. But whether the psychological derivation is valid or not isn't so important. The reality is maintained even without a "why" to explain it. And the reality for me is that I cannot, without feeling sudden pangs of revulsion, kiss someone to whom I am not deeply attached. When I *am* that attached, a kiss reverberates with all of the delicacy of a moment at once complete and expectant, reaching forward into remote territories of sexual exploration, balancing tenderness and passion. Kisses are fine things . . . and rare enough in that form.

For a relatively brief period in my life, I believed, as some feminists now do, that selective promiscuity was a means of resolving some of the conflicts of love. I would have agreed with Germaine Greer that monogamy would be a "fluke" in a truly free society. It seemed to me then that the best way not to invest too much in a relationship with one man, and the best way to avoid being hurt, was to love a lot of men; if I wished to protect myself against my own intensity, my natural drift toward exclusivity, then I should learn to spread myself around and thus avoid being a burden to myself or anyone else; if I didn't want to get my thorns stuck in the thick hide of male polygamy, then I too should become polygamous. So, on occasion, spurred by an instantaneous attraction, or a friendship that seemed to demand such an attraction, I would "decide" to sleep with someone, thinking that the interest and the attraction would mesh naturally with the sex since they presumably belonged together in the first place. Except, as in the situation with my Greek friend, this "meshing" almost never took place. Either my body refused to cooperate with my mind, or my mind refused to cooperate with my body. The conglomerate merger was invariably a failure, demanding a more skillful management than I was capable of providing. Sometimes I would say to myself. "All right now, just relax and let go," and then watch my body as it rolled away down the steep incline of an opposite impulse. I would reach out my hand and see it draw back of its own accord. Or else I would go ahead with the "act" (for me, such situations always had a theatrical element to them), feel myself on the verge of an orgasm, and suddenly, without having consciously decided anything, I would be unable to show that I was responding. The orgasm would pass without a trace. Something in me refused to allow a man possession of something so deep in me unless my feelings were equally deep . . . not necessarily that I was in love with him, but close enough to it that I could feel the potential for love creating itself on some embryonic scale. I might have an orgasm with someone I didn't love. But I couldn't share an orgasm. My will revolted. My body, of course, was still sufficiently instinctual that it responded to the stimulus. But the mere fact that physical instincts push you in a particular direction does not mean that direction is basically satisfying. We are complicated creatures, and human life defines itself along the knife edge of its own contradictions.

I have heard of women supposedly capable of having an orgasm while being raped. A man once used that as evidence of women's secret pleasure in the attack—except having an orgasm does not necessarily represent the same thing to a woman as it does to a man. A woman can have an orgasm and still hate the man who raped her, because physical response is meaningless to many women when they can't link it up with emotional response. Certainly a part of us, the purely physical part, can respond to something purely physical. But our sexual capacities very often exceed our capacities for human engagement on other levels, and our bodies grow parched in the wasteland between.

The issue of multiple relationships is not a moral one: it is an emotional one . . . as well as a practical one (more on that later). It is no less moral for women to have multiple love affairs than it is for men to have them. But my own experience tells me that even if society were to declare that I was entitled to go fifty-fifty with a man on the number of love affairs we were allowed to indulge in simultaneously, I would never make use of my share, simply because the varieties of sexual experience, in themselves, are not enough to draw me into bed with someone . . .

because sex is always a deeply revealing matter and I prefer not to reveal myself that much to that many people (even if I were capable of it, which I'm not) . . . because I have friends I love but have very little sexual feeling for . . . because my sexual and emotional energies, even when they are distributed among several people, tend to concentrate themselves more exclusively toward one person.

The question then becomes more directly one of: do multiple love affairs satisfy our needs? If they do, fine. I have no doubt that they satisfy the needs of some women, and those women are no better and no worse than I am. There is little point, however, in creating false solutions to real problems, and those of us who are *not* satisfied by multiplicity are still left with the difficulty of adapting ourselves to the fact that men, on the contrary, usually seem more inclined to multiple relationships than we are, to sex for its own sake rather than sex as an expression of more complicated impulses. How do we acknowledge the disparities in our needs, while neither shattering the requirements of intimacy, nor imposing our values on another, nor feeling cheated or betrayed or belittled? How deal with the fact that although "sharing" is theoretically a question of mutual concern, it is more often a question of your willingness to share him, rather than his willingness to share you, since you rarely have much desire for anyone else, and might be able to trump up such a desire only for the sake of the argument, for the sake of not being in a position where his freedom is your bondage. Say to me, "You are free to do as you wish," and I will do what

I have done all along, that is, be inclined toward one man in most situations. Say to him, "You are free to do as you wish," and usually he, too, will do what he has done all along, that is, be inclined toward several women.

A number of women I know (including myself) decided at one time or another that the only workable solution was to remain faithful themselves (at least until or unless they had a genuine desire to be with someone else) and adapt to the "diversity" of attachments to which the men they loved were inclined. It was pointless to "forbid" a man to make love with other women and just as pointless to forbid him to fall in love with another woman. Honesty compelled a frank admission of his other interests . . . honesty and the fear that if you didn't know about it, it might slip beyond the boundaries of your eagle-eyed gaze and transform itself into something more threatening than you wanted it to be. How many times did I listen dispassionately to a man as he told me that he was attracted to another woman, how many times swallow the dread that she might usurp my place in his life? But making love meant so many diverse things to me that I never could assimilate the idea that it might mean less to him: and if it did mean less, then I was distressed over his involvement in "meaningless sex," although if it meant just as much, I was distressed by the thought that another woman could be as important to him as I was. What guarantee did I have that she would not become *more* important, that I would not suddenly be confronted with a *fait accompli?* Theoretically, of course, that was all unimportant, except my image of myself was never so grand that

I was able to assume the advantages of my own merits to the merits of another woman. I couldn't stop him from having love affairs, but neither could I stop myself from being afraid of the threat they represented to my happiness. I didn't want him to lie to me, but I also couldn't pretend to be unaffected by the truth. If he was away on a trip and a chance encounter took place, I was undisturbed. If he met an old friend and they wound up in bed together, I was also undisturbed. Single, isolated incidents were not threatening. They could be attributed to an impulse, a momentary desire. But once an impulse was repeated or pursued, its character changed. It became a new relationship, and therefore dangerous.

Certainly it's true that additional relationships often enrich marriages and love affairs, restore freshness to them or restore appreciations that have evaporated. The only problem is that one never *knows* that that's what's going to happen. One hopes that the "intruder" or "intruders" will do their job of enrichment and retire from the scene eventually . . . though often, in the middle of the night, one's body shrinks away with fear at the comparison, one doubts, hesitates, withdraws. One is terrified. There are cold sweats to contend with, and the comfort of his presence next to you is no comfort at all, even though you think fleetingly that it is still preferable to have him beside you than beside someone else.

The question of whom he spends the night next to is, finally, of crucial importance—practical importance as well as emotional importance. Our theoretical model for the future usually manages to ignore the fact that committed people devote about half of their waking hours to whatever they are committed to, that even for those who have no commitments, there are still only twenty-four hours in a day, a third of which are spent sleeping, fifty-two weekends (even if they are three-day weekends) in a year, one month (if you're lucky) of vacation time, and about five long holiday weekends. Not only that, but Christmas and New Year's come only once a year, as do birthdays.

Having been on the less cheerful side of that estimate, I know how crucial such "innocent facts" can become. One or the other of you is going to spend the night with him, the weekend with him, Christmas with him. (I've tried all three of us spending it together. Doesn't work.) One or the other of you is going to go on trips with him.

Sooner or later, one becomes competitive about such a simple thing as time, human time. I want it; she wants it; we're both entitled to it. I have a busy day; she has a busy day; he has a busy day. Maybe there are four or five of us and we all have busy days. Our time for loving is limited to the nights . . . or at least evenings and nights, although one or the other of us might be willing to settle for the lunchtime slot. Two hours though and presto; back to the world of art and science and social change. The thought makes me gag; I've been there, and it made me gag then, too.

If you're the wife or the woman he lives with, the woman he "comes home to," you become increasingly aware that he's never at home . . . or that he arrives at midnight glowing with an unexpected warmth and affection that you know you've done nothing to provoke. (Such bursts of affection from men who are just returning from a few hours with another woman are so common that one would wish to tell them how obvious and predictable it is, even as one recognizes how pleased with themselves they are for being able to "conceal" it.) Usually, he manages to love you all the more for having been with her, though something in you stiffens, even as you say to yourself defensively, "Well, I should be glad he's here at all."

If you're the woman he doesn't live with, the woman he goes away from home for, you become increasingly aware that he leaves you every time at midnight, says "I love you," and disappears down the street, or that the connection between your phone and his is broken between the hours of midnight and nine a.m.

No matter who you are, or where you stand in the relationship, invariably there are problems too complex to handle gracefully. Personally, I find it confusing, to say the least, to wake up to three different people in the course of a week, and do not look forward with any great anticipation to waking up to listen to the person beside me call out someone else's name from the center of his erotically charged dream. Nor would I like to be the one doing the calling out. I am embarrassed enough by the fact that sometimes when I was having sex with one person, my imagination transported me far enough afield that I thought I was with someone I cared for more deeply.

That's multiplicity, unless of course, you all live separately, spend impossible periods of time on the subways, rotate who sleeps where (everyone in the spirit of true generosity sacrificing his or her desires to the desires of the other), and are capable of breezily claiming that you wanted to spend the night alone anyway, even though the night you wanted to spend alone was last night, and the night he wants to spend alone or with her is tonight. Of course no one *dies* of despair over such arrangements; we struggle through them trying to find some sort of modus vivendi. But I suspect most women who claim to be genuinely satisfied with "sharing" are usually lying. In the majority of cases it is a matter of settling for the possible, of sacrificing one need for the sake of another, of sharing simply because you'd rather have something than nothing.

Of course, you can all try living together (communally perhaps) and stumbling over each other's embraces in the middle of the kitchen, not batting an eyelash and having morbid fantasies about it afterward in the privacy of your own room (if you have an own room) or else "discussing" it intelligently together, and *then* having morbid fantasies. Sex is just sex, you say, knowing that, in fact, it's dynamite. So you try a ménage once or twice. I tried it once and though in many ways I enjoyed it, since I was stoned and my puritan tendencies simply evaporated, I was finally forced to confront a problem of simple mathematics: one penis can't fit into two vaginas simultaneously, and timing being a matter of no small importance, that made quite a difference. Although I bowed out gracefully and settled for voyeurism, I can't say that I found the experience all that satisfying, since I still preferred things on a simple one-to-one basis. Men, it seems, prefer ménages that consist of two women and one man, since the opportunities for them are more various, and when one hears accounts of two men and one woman, it is usually in association either with a rape scene or with some "wildly insatiable woman intoxicated with the . . ." I know that this is not always the case, but the literature, produced as it is by males and therefore a product of male fantasies, does not give us much enlightenment on other kinds of needs. I, for one, have no inclination in that direction, and can supply nothing in the way of perspectives. Still, it seems to me that the whole thing too easily devolves into sexual games, and since physical thrills are not the issue, we might as well go on to other things.

Of course, there are an infinite number of ways in which multiple relationships can be approached. Sometimes they even work, for a while. But invariably someone's needs increase, someone becomes more attached, someone simply falls in love and wants more than what she or he is theoretically entitled to. Shares can never be parceled out fairly enough to take into account the slow crescendoing of human desires and expectations. No matter how sensible one may be, no matter how committed to the sexual revolution, life eludes the formulas with which we would attempt to enclose it.

I have noticed among those of my female friends who are inclined toward multiple relationships, and are capable of sustaining them, that even if *their* needs don't multiply, the needs of the men who surround them do. It is precisely those women who tend to attract men devoted exclusively to them, just as men who prefer multiplicity attract devoted women. Someone, it seems, has to provide the cement if the whole thing is not to go whirling off into the stratosphere of an intoxicating—though largely deceptive—freedom. Someone's ego, finally, always winds up at the center of things.

That, however, is not the crucial point. What really counts most is the fact that the majority of people still make such distinctions as "good-better-best" and don't separate their needs neatly enough so it is possible for them to say, "X satisfies my need for stability, Y my need for wildness, Z my need for brilliance and eccentricity," without also eventually getting caught up in the sense that "X, although satisfying my need for stability, is otherwise quite boring, while Y, who satisfies my need for wildness, completely lacks sensitivity to my needs as a whole person, and Z, who satisfies my need for brilliance and eccentricity, is so brilliant and eccentric that the time I spend with him is thoroughly exhausting." Since we are all limited human beings, we try to satisfy as many needs as possible in one person, because we usually wind up feeling that the parceling-out involved in caring deeply for X, Y and Z brings us face to face with our own parsimony as well as theirs. No matter how much equality can be achieved in other areas, there is and always will be such a thing as inequality on the emotional scale.

It is conceivable, of course, that the idea of sharing would become more satisfying if everyone got his or her fair share, but unfortunately, one almost never does. Many of the women I know whose husbands or lovers are exclusively "devoted" to them are frustrated at how little such devotion provides in the way of satisfactions. If you have very little to give in the first place, you're not going to have more to give when you divide it up among three or four or five people. It's hard enough to convince a man of the value of making one affectionate phone call a day, let alone try to convince him that he should be capable of making five, hard enough to get him to open up sufficiently that he is willing to even admit that loving is *as* important as work (not more important, just as important) without expecting him to be capable of dividing up what is left of himself after work among five women—and doing it well. If "the little things" seem too little to warrant his attention with one woman, how on earth are they going to warrant his attention with several? If it takes years to break down the barriers of his resistance to revealing himself as something less than a Knight of the Round Table, years to establish authenticity between the two of you, how will he achieve that authenticity in an instant with a slew of other people? (Some would say that authenticity is contagious, that if you are open with one person, you can be open with anyone, but whether or not one is capable of being open, the situations in which it isn't dangerous are relatively few and far between. Authentic openness is too volatile a commodity to be distributed easily. People build defenses in order to survive, and not simply for their own pleasure.)

How will he do and be all of these things? How will I? For if love is work, then where on earth is either of us going to find the time to do that much work with more than one person simultaneously? Frankly, I am not too confident of either my ability or his ability (whoever he is) to love anyone, let alone love ten people. I run hot and cold with infuriating regularity (even if my conditioning has produced that state, it is no easier to live with), and have a list of compulsions to delight the connoisseur. My daily life resembles a battlefield of conflicting emotions. Although I am interested only in what is intense, I am exhausted by intensity. I want to draw some pure gold out of love and life, but am forced to acknowledge that, likely as not, I would think it was counterfeit if someone dumped a truckload in my living room.

All in all, then, I am not too sure whether my inventory of personal resources leaves me in the red or the black, and know that, unfortunately, the inventory doesn't substantially change my dealings with one person or another. I would be more than happy to succeed in disposing of my hangups with one person, and, if I could, I would not very likely want to share that person with too many others.

Most of the people I know have similar inventories, though the items vary considerably. Our best impulses mutate into their opposites the moment we turn our backs on Cynthia Superstar. When I think of the amount of sheer repetition involved in loving several men and/or women (since I am not so various that I can love five people in five stunningly original ways), my imagination begins to stagger. The stop-start quality of it all is enough to make my psyche ragged with dissatisfaction. In the process of keeping track of the ins and outs of all their lives, of the events that contributed to their mood of today (since I haven't seen them for two weeks, it takes a few hours to catch up to where they are), I all too easily get lost myself. If I feel capable of expending enough tenderness and concern and interest and enthusiasm and warmth to satisfy the minimum daily requirements of all the people I love within the course of one week (assuming that I am not the only one attempting to satisfy their needs), I will more than likely be in a comatose state the following week. Personally, I have a limited supply of psychic commodities, and a good portion of them are used up in the process of trying to sustain *myself.*

There is something comforting, then, about being in the regular presence of one person who can adapt to varying dosages of your capacities and incapacities and for whom you can do the same. The thought of loving someone whom you can see for four or five hours every day and spend the night with, sharing the daily accumulation of simple, silent warmth, both sexual and nonsexual, is one of the more inspiring aspects of life, whenever it can be achieved.

Such thoughts put me in the category of being a fairly possessive human being, which I am. And if nothing else, that would make me unfit for multiple relations. But even if possessiveness is a taboo, I would hope and expect that someone I loved would be somewhat possessive about me too, though not obsessively so. Being possessive about one's happiness is a natural thing—especially since there's so little of it around. One would be crazy to give away what has been achieved with so much effort in the first place.

. . .

Permanence in love, of course, is just about impossible to achieve. But that doesn't make it any less desirable. It's impossible to achieve immortality too, but no one would suggest that we should simply forget about the fact that we are perishable creatures. Thoughts about permanence are an integral part of life, and the need of people to create *something* permanent, whether it be a building or a business with their name attached to it, a child who carries some part of them into the future, a painting or a book, has haunted the human imagination throughout history. The only thing permanent about love, though, is the persistence with which we seek it, and even if there is little comfort to be gained from the fact that we can't achieve it, there might be some comfort in the thought that we share our concern about it with every society, every culture that has ever existed. Primitive tribesmen bewail the loss of love as much as the Chinese revolutionaries in *Man's Fate,* and each society has its antidotes to the pains associated with the loss of love, whether they include the carrying of talismans to prevent it, or the construction of rules for social and antisocial behavior which make it counterrevolutionary to love one person too long and too deeply.

I am obsessive about the problem and cannot be relied upon for any objectivity. Despite my firm belief in the importance of living "in the moment," every time I begin a relationship, I have to overcome my considerable sense of dread about the likelihood of its ending—not exactly what one would call a "healthy attitude," but a real one, nonetheless.

I imagine that anyone who has lived in the stultifying environment of a suburban tract for twenty years, lived with someone she or he has found increasingly uninteresting over a quarter of a century, or held a particularly boring job for a great length of time, finds the problem of permanence rather dull.

But those of us who have lived differently, as I have, consider it a matter of crucial importance. An orphan cares more deeply about having a home than children with parents who have lived on vast estates most of their lives. Someone whose marriage or affair has just ended is more aware of, and more disturbed by, the problem of duration than someone whose marriage has endured so long that it has become impossibly sickening. Probably everyone basically needs a home and various kinds of security. It is just that we are reactive beings, and our priorities establish themselves according to our experiences. Human beings become most conscious of their own needs when those needs are not being met, and evolve other needs when they are.

"Nothing lasts . . . everything perishes" is the cry of people who have lived intimately with death or destruction, loss or desertion, although it is very often precisely those people who most determinedly try to confront the problems of evanescence, disintegration, and life's unpredictability. Camus, who insisted emphatically on the need for facing the "benign indifference of the universe" to human fate and the human need for unity, was one of them, and his notebooks are filled with the anguish of a man who could scarcely bear the fact of transience in life or in love.

I am always astounded when philosophers of the movement talk blithely about the "ideal of uprootedness"—the freedom to move around—and express contempt for the apparent lack of originality in the lives of people who have struggled for stability and permanence. I am equally astounded when serial relationships are proposed as quick solutions to human misery, as if to suggest that the transition from one relationship to another could be made "naturally." It's not possible, even if one of the persons, or both, are looking forward to a "new beginning" with someone else. Of course it's true that people develop differently, and that one of the consequences of these differences is that people who once had a great deal in common discover that they no longer have anything in common. The only "reasonable" thing to do then is terminate the relationship. But no one with any sensitivity manages to get over that hurdle without being at some time or another excruciatingly aware of what it means to have spent five or ten or twenty years with someone accustomed to your idiosyncrasies, familiar with the patterns of your thoughts, and willing to put up with you at those moments when you were fighting against your worst (but nonetheless *known*) self.

I've had several long love affairs. I've escaped from the sheer misery involved in their ending by moving to another part of the world . . . a year in Greece, a year in

Israel, six months in Paris, several months in Holland, several in Mexico . . . or working to the point of exhaustion, or sleeping an inordinate number of hours a day, or going into seclusion for long periods of time. I relived memories and disdained to relive them. I said, "That's life"; or, "Well, at least if I've done a lot of running it's been interesting running"; or, "But look how much I've *done* that I would never have done if . . ."; and then, in the privacy of my apartment, lay awake nights thinking about what all the "doing" amounted to, thinking that, yes, I was happy that I'd seen the world, but, no, it was not enough to do that, not enough at all . . . not, I thought, for anyone.

If given the choice I would prefer not to go through any more endings, even though I know that the nature of human relations being what it is, sooner or later the odds are that I will have to.

Recently I had a long talk with my twenty-four-year-old brother, who had returned only a few months before from a trip to India, where he had spent five months meditating in a mountain village at the foot of the Himalayas. He was thinking of getting married to a woman he'd known for about three years. My immediate reaction, of course, was, "But Steven, how *could* you. You're so young and marriage is so *permanent.* Why don't you at least wait until you want to have children and just keep on living together."

"It's so easy to do that," he said. "You can live with someone and move out anytime . . . whenever it gets rough. We already *know* we can live together. I don't see any reason to stay in the same stage all of the time, and marriage is another stage. There's a difference."

I was about to say, "Of course there's a difference . . . and that's why you should keep on living together," but then an old image passed through my mind, and I realized how quickly one could deny the evidence of one's own experience.

The image was of a hotel near a railroad station in a small town on the Austrian-Italian border. I was sitting out on the patio drinking *caffe latte* with a recently divorced painter. We had been living together in Greece for some time and I was on my way back to the States. He was on his way back to his home in Austria. We were spending a last weekend together before separating. It was a weekend of being in love and making plans. The plans included his coming to America several months later . . . maybe.

"Three months together, three months apart," he said. "That will keep things fresh. You'll do your work and I'll do mine. The time will go very fast. And then we'll be together again."

"Yes," I said, "I suppose so," and felt something drop inside of me like a stone falling down an elevator shaft.

"One thing is sure. I never want to be married again."

"Never?" I said.

"No, never."

"What about children? Don't you ever want to have children?"

"No."

"Oh."

It had been a long time since the subject had come up. The last time we'd talked about marriage I had agreed with him . . . marriage was a trap . . . it took the spontaneity out of life. Now I wasn't so sure. There was something so final about the word "never." It was like looking down a tunnel that got progressively darker instead of moving up toward the light. It was a dead-end word. But wasn't "marriage" also a dead-end word? Suddenly it didn't seem to be . . . in an instant, my perspective had shifted almost imperceptibly. A theory had been transformed into a reality, wedged now between two words.

"How can you say 'never' about something? Life is always changing. You can't know how you're going to feel a year from now about anything."

"I know. I've been through it once and I don't want to go through it again."

"But that's so static. I think maybe someday I would want to be married and have children. I don't know for sure, but I certainly couldn't say 'never.' Why say it? Can't you just leave things open and see what happens?"

"Look," he said, "there isn't any point in talking about it now, is there? We're not thinking of getting married, so why discuss it?"

"We don't have to discuss it. I just don't like the sound of the word 'never.' "

"All right then," he said. Then he laughed and kissed me. But he didn't retract the "never."

I was twenty-two then. For the next year and a half we lived out our ultra-contemporary arrangement . . . together three months, apart three months. We flew back and forth across two continents. At first I thought it was very romantic. Then I began to think that it really ought to be more romantic than it was. I wasn't feeling spontaneous and fresh because of being apart for so long. In fact, if anything, I was feeling much less spontaneous, since it always took me several weeks to adjust to our being together or being apart. Continuity, it seemed, might be what made spontaneity possible in the first place.

After the year and a half was over, we split up. I didn't understand why we had to do that. I wanted to keep on working at things. He didn't. Suddenly I realized that we had been so concerned with maintaining freshness that we had forgotten all about laying foundations and building with cement.

It took me well over a year to get over that. There were times when I wondered what would have happened if we had got married. Would we have been divorced by now? Would we have worked our way through the difficulties and come out with something stronger, richer, more dense and complex? It was impossible to know. Still . . .

Recently, I have become aware of the marriage contracts that many feminists are drawing up . . . contracts that guarantee women their "rights" . . . including the right to live separate lives whenever the women want to.

It makes me think about what a funny concept "rights" is, and about contracts that presumably can guarantee them. What about the fact that everything ever constructed by civilization seems to be a dam against disintegration? I think about my brother, about how similar words like "never" and "forever" are. And I wonder about having to walk such very thin lines.